Book 3

MAXIMIZE YOUR POTENTIAL

THROUGH THE POWER OF

YOUR SUBCONSCIOUS MIND

TO DEVELOP

Self-Confidence

and Self-Esteem

Book 3

MAXIMIZE YOUR POTENTIAL

THROUGH THE POWER OF

YOUR SUBCONSCIOUS MIND

TO DEVELOP

Self-Confidence
and Self-Esteem

One of a Series of Six Books
by
Dr. Joseph Murphy

Edited and Updated for the 21st Century
by Arthur R. Pell, Ph.D.

HAY HOUSE, INC.
Carlsbad, California • New York City
London • Sydney • Johannesburg
Vancouver • Hong Kong • New Delhi

DR. JOSEPH MURPHY

Maximize Your Potential Through the Power of Your Subconscious Mind to Develop Self-Confidence and Self-Esteem, one of a series of six books by Joseph Murphy, D.D., Ph.D. Edited and updated for the 21st century by Arthur R. Pell, Ph.D. Copyright © 2005 The James A. Boyer Revocable Trust. Exclusive worldwide rights in all languages available only through JMW Group Inc.

Published and distributed in the United States by: Hay House, Inc.: www.hay house.com • **Published and distributed in Australia by:** Hay House Australia Pty. Ltd.: www.hayhouse.com.au • **Published and distributed in the United Kingdom by:** Hay House UK, Ltd.: www.hayhouse.co.uk • **Published and distributed in the Republic of South Africa by:** Hay House SA (Pty), Ltd.: www.hayhouse.co.za • **Distributed in Canada by:** Raincoast: www.raincoast.com • **Published in India by:** Hay House Publishers India: www.hayhouse.co.in

Library of Congress Cataloging-in-Publication Data

Murphy, Joseph.
    Maximize your potential through the power of your subconscious mind to develop self-confidence and self-esteem / by Joseph Murphy ; edited and updated for the 21st century by Arthur R. Pell. -- 1st Hay House ed.
    p. cm. -- (Maximize your potential series ; bk. 3)
    ISBN-13: 978-1-4019-1216-1 (tradepaper) 1. New Thought. I. Pell, Arthur R. II. Title.
    BF639.M8317 2008
    154.2--dc22   2006031170

ISBN: 978-1-4019-1216-1

11 10 09 08   5 4 3 2
1st Hay House edition, February 2008
2nd Hay House edition, August 2008

Printed in the United States of America

CONTENTS

—

Introduction to the Series

*W*ake up and live! No one is destined to be unhappy or consumed with fear and worry, live in poverty, suffer ill health, and feel rejected and inferior. God created all humans in His image and has given us the power to overcome adversity and attain happiness, harmony, health, and prosperity.

You have within you the power to enrich your life! How to do this is no secret. It has been preached, written about, and practiced for millennia. You will find it in the works of the ancient philosophers, and all of the great religions have preached it. It is in the Hebrew scriptures, the Christian Gospels, Greek philosophy, the Muslim Koran, the Buddhist sutras, the Hindu Bhagavad Gita, and the writings of Confucius and Lao-tzu. You will find it in the works of modern psychologists and theologians.

This is the basis of the philosophy of Dr. Joseph Murphy, one of the great inspirational writers and lecturers of the 20th century. He was not just a clergyman, but also a major figure in the modern interpretation of scriptures and other religious writings. As minister-director of the Church of Divine Science in Los Angeles, his lectures and sermons were attended by 1,300 to 1,500 people every Sunday, and millions tuned in to his daily radio program. He wrote more than 30 books, and his most well-known one, *The Power of Your Subconscious Mind,* was first published in 1963 and became an immediate bestseller. It was acclaimed as one of the greatest self-help guides ever written. Millions of copies have, and continue to be, sold all over the world.

Following the success of this book, Dr. Murphy lectured to audiences of thousands in several countries. In his lectures he pointed out how real people have radically improved their lives by applying specific aspects of his concepts, and he provided practical guidelines on how all people can enrich themselves.

Dr. Murphy was a proponent of the New Thought movement, which was developed in the late 19th and early 20th century by many philosophers and deep thinkers who studied it and preached, wrote, and practiced a new way of looking at life. By combining metaphysical, spiritual, and pragmatic approaches to the way we think and live, they uncovered the secret for attaining what we truly desire.

This philosophy wasn't a religion in the traditional sense, but it was based on an unconditional belief in a higher being, an eternal presence: God. It was called by various names, such as "New Thought" and "New Civilization."

The proponents of New Thought or New Civilization preached a fresh idea of life that makes use of methods that lead to perfected results. They based their thinking on the concept that the human soul is connected with the atomic mind of universal substance, which links our lives with the universal law of supply, and we have the power to use it to enrich our lives. To achieve our goals, we must work, and through this working, we may suffer the thorns and heartaches of humankind. We can do all these things only as we have found the law and worked out an understanding of the principles that God seemed to have written in riddles in the past.

The New Thought concept can be summed up in these words:

You can become what you want to be.

All that we achieve and all that we fail to achieve is the direct result of our own thoughts. In a just and ordered universe, where loss of balance would mean total destruction, individual responsibility must be absolute. Our weaknesses, strengths, purity, and impurity are ours alone. They are brought about by ourselves and not by another. They can only be altered by ourselves, and never by anyone else. All of our happiness and suffering evolve from within. As we think, so we are; as we continue to think, so we remain. The only way we can rise, conquer, and achieve is by lifting up our thoughts. The only reason we may remain weak, abject, and miserable is to *refuse* to elevate our minds.

All achievements—whether in the business, intellectual, or spiritual world—are the result of definitely directed thought; and are governed by the same law and are reached by the same method. The only difference lies in the object of attainment. Those who would accomplish little must sacrifice little; those who would achieve much must sacrifice much; those who would attain a great deal must sacrifice a great deal.

New Thought means a new life: a way of living that is healthier, happier, and more fulfilling in every possible manner and expression.

Actually, there is nothing new in this, for it is as old and time-honored as humankind. It is novel to us when we discover the truths of life that set us free from lack, limitation, and unhappiness. At that moment, New Thought becomes a recurring, expanding awareness of the creative power within; of mind-principle; and of our Divine potential to be, to do, and to express more of our individual and natural abilities, aptitudes, and talents. The central mind-principle is that new thoughts, ideas, attitudes, and beliefs create new conditions. According to our beliefs, is it done unto us—good, bad, or indifferent. The essence of New Thought consists of the continual renewing of our mind, that we may manifest what is good, acceptable, and the perfect will of God.

To prove is to know surely, and to have trustworthy knowledge and experience. The truths of New Thought are practical, easy to demonstrate, and within the realm of accomplishment of everyone—if and when he or she chooses. All that is required is an open mind and a willing heart: open to hearing old truths presented in a different way; willing to change and to relinquish outmoded beliefs and to accept unfamiliar ideas and concepts—to have a higher vision of life, or a healing presence within.

The rebirth of our mind constitutes the entire purpose and practice of New Thought. Without this ongoing daily renewal, there can be no change. New Thought establishes and realizes an entirely new attitude and consciousness that inspires and enables us to enter into "life more abundant."

We have within us limitless powers to choose and to decide, and complete freedom to be conformed or to be transformed. To be conformed is to live according to that which already has taken or been given form—that which is visible and apparent to our own senses, including the ideas, opinions, beliefs, and edicts of others. It is to live and to be governed "by the fleeting and unstable fashions and conditions of the moment." The very word *conformed* suggests that our present environment has shape, and that we do not and should not deny its existence. All around us there are injustices, improprieties, and inequalities. We may and do find ourselves involved in them at times, and we should face them with courage and honesty and do our best to resolve them with the integrity and intelligence that we now possess.

Generally, the world accepts and believes that our environment is the cause of our present condition and circumstance—and the usual reaction and tendency is to drift into a state of acquiescence and quiet acceptance of the present. This is conformity of the worst kind: the consciousness of defeatism. It's worse because it is self-imposed. It is giving all power and attention to the outer, manifested state. New Thought insists on the renewal of the mind, and the recognition and acknowledgment of our responsibility in life—our ability to respond to the truths we now know.

One of the most active and effective of New Thought teachers, Charles Fillmore, co-founder of the Unity School of Christianity, was a firm believer in personal responsibility. In his book *The Revealing Word,* he wrote (simply, and without equivocation): "Our consciousness is our real environment. The outer environment is always in correspondence to our consciousness."

Anyone who is open and willing to accept the responsibility has begun the transformation—the renewal of the mind that enables us to participate in our transformed life. "To transform" is "to change from one condition or state to another" (which is qualitatively better and more fulfilling) "from lack to abundance; loneliness to companionship; limitation to fullness; illness to vibrant health"—through this indwelling wisdom and power, the healing presence will remain within.

True and granted, there are some things we cannot change: the movement of the planets, the turn of the seasons, the pull of the oceans and tides, and the apparent rising and setting of the sun. Neither can we alter the minds and thoughts of another person—but we can change ourselves.

Who can prevent or inhibit the movement of your imagination and will? Only you can give that power to another. You can be transformed by the renewing of your mind. This is the key to a new life. You're a recording machine; and all the beliefs, impressions, opinions, and ideas accepted by you are impressed in your deeper subconscious. But you can change. You can begin now to fill your mind with noble and Godlike patterns of thoughts, and align yourself with the Infinite Spirit within. Claim beauty, love, peace, wisdom, creative ideas . . . and the Infinite will respond accordingly, transforming your mind, body, and circumstances. Your thought is the medium between your spirit, your body, and the material world.

The transformation begins as we meditate, think upon, and absorb into our mentality those qualities that we desire to experience and express. Theoretical knowledge is good and necessary. We should understand what we're doing and why. However, actual change depends entirely on stirring up the gifts within—the invisible and intangible spiritual power given fully to every one of us.

This, and only this, ultimately breaks up and dissolves the very real claims and bondage of past unhappiness and distress. In addition, it heals the wounds of heartbreak and emotional pain. We all desire and require peace of mind—the greatest gift—in order to bring it into our environment. Mentally and emotionally, contemplate Divine peace, filling our mind and heart, our entire being. First say, "Peace be unto this house."

To contemplate lack of peace, disharmony, unhappiness, and discord, and expect peace to manifest is to expect the apple seed to grow into a pear. It makes little or no sense, and it violates all sense of reason, but it is the way of the world. We must seek ways to change our minds—to repent where necessary. As a result, renewal will occur, following naturally. It is desirable and necessary to transform our lives by ceasing to conform to the world's way of choosing or deciding, according to the events already formed and manifested.

The word *metaphysical* has become a synonym for the modern, organized movement. It was first used by Aristotle. Considered by some to have been his greatest writing, his 13th volume was simply entitled *Metaphysics.* The dictionary definition is: "Beyond natural science; the science of pure being." *Meta-* means "above, or beyond." *Metaphysics,* then, means "above or beyond physics"— "above or beyond the physical," the world of form. "Meta" is above that; it is the spirit of the mind, which is behind all things.

Biblically, the spirit of God is good. "They that worship God worship the spirit, or truth." When we have the spirit of goodness, truth, beauty, love, and goodwill, it is actually the Divine in us, moving through us. God, truth, life, energy, spirit—can it not be defined? How can it be? "To define it is to limit it."

This is expressed in a beautiful old meditation:

> *Ever the same in my innermost being: eternal, absolutely one, whole, complete, perfect; I AM indivisible, timeless, shapeless, ageless—without face, form, or figure. I AM the silent brooding presence, fixed in the hearts of all men (and women).*

We must believe and accept that whatever we imagine and feel to be true will come to pass; whatever we desire for another, we are wishing for ourselves.

Emerson wrote: "We become what we think about all day long." In other words and most simply stated: Spirit, thought, mind, and meta is the expression of creative presence and power—and as in nature (physical laws), any force can be used two ways. For example, water can clean us or drown us; electricity can make life easier or more deadly. The Bible says: "I form the light, and create darkness; I make peace, and evil; I, the Lord, do all these things—I wound, I heal; I bless, I curse."

No angry deity is punishing us; we punish ourselves by misuse of the mind. We also are blessed (benefited) when we comprehend this fundamental principle and presence, and learn and accept a new thought or an entire concept.

Metaphysics, then, is the study of causation—concerned not with the effect that is now manifest, but rather with that which is causing the result. This discipline approaches spiritual ideas as scientists approach the world of form, just as they investigate the mind or causation from which the visible is formed, or derived. If a mind is changed, or a cause is changed, the effect is changed.

The strength and beauty of metaphysics, in my opinion, is that it is not confined to any one particular creed, but is universal. One can be a Jew, Christian, Muslim, or Buddhist and yet still be a metaphysician.

There are poets, scientists, and philosophers who claim no creed; their belief is metaphysical.

Jesus was a master metaphysician—he understood the mind and employed it to lift up, inspire, and heal others.

When Mahatma Gandhi (the "great-souled" one) was asked what his religion was, he replied, "I am a Christian . . . a Jew . . . a Buddhist . . . a Hindu . . . I AM all these things."

The term *New Thought* has become a popular, generalized term. Composed of a very large number of churches, centers, prayer groups, and institutions, this has become a metaphysical movement that reveals the oneness or unity of humankind with Infinite life . . . with the innate dignity, worth, or value of every individual. In fact, and in truth, the emphasis is on the individual rather than on an organizational body or function. But as mentioned, there is nothing new in New Thought. Metaphysics is actually the oldest of all religious approaches. It reveals our purpose to express God, and the greater measures of the Good: "I AM come to bring you life and that more abundantly." It reveals our identity: "children of the infinite" who are loved and have spiritual value as necessary parts of the Creative Holy (whole) One.

Metaphysics enables and assists us to return to our Divine Source, and ends the sense of separation and feeling of alienation; of wandering in a barren, unfriendly desert wasteland. This approach has always been, is now, and ever will be available to all—patiently waiting our discovery and revelation.

Many thousands have been introduced to New Thought through one or another of its advocates. Its formation was gradual, and usually considered to have begun with Phineas P. Quimby. In a fascinating article in *New Thought* magazine, Quimby wrote about his work in 1837. After experimenting with mesmerism for a period of years, he concluded that it was not the hypnotism itself, but the conditioning of the subconscious, which led to the resulting changes. Although Quimby had very little formal education, he had a brilliant, investigative mind and was an original thinker. In addition, he was a prolific writer and diarist. Records have been published detailing the development of his findings. He eventually became a wonderful student of the Bible and duplicated two-thirds of the Old and New Testament healings. He found that there was much confusion about the true meaning of many biblical passages, which caused misunderstanding and misinterpretation of Jesus Christ.

All through the 20th century, so many inspired teachers, authors, ministers, and lecturers contributed to the New Thought movement. Dr. Charles E. Braden, of the University of Chicago, called these people "spirits in rebellion" because these men and women were truly breaking free from existing dogmatism, rituals, and creeds. (Rebelling at inconsistencies in the old traditions led some individuals to fear religion.) Dr. Braden became discontent with the status quo and refused to conform any longer.

New Thought is an individual practice of the truths of life—a gradual, continuing process. We can learn a bit today, and even more tomorrow. Never will we experience a point where there is nothing more to be discovered. It is infinite, boundless, and eternal. We have all the time we need—eternity. Many of us are impatient with ourselves, and with what we consider our failures. Looking back, though, we discover that these have been periods of learning, and we needn't make these mistakes again. Progress may seem ever so slow: "In patience, possess ye your soul."

In Dr. Murphy's book *Pray Your Way Through It: The Revelation*, he commented that heaven was noted as being "awareness," and Earth, "manifestation." Your new heaven is your revised point of view—your new dimension of consciousness. When we see—that is, see *spiritually*, we then realize that in the absolute, all is blessed, harmony, boundless love, wisdom, complete peace, and perfection. Identify with these truths, calm the sea of fear; have confidence and faith, and become stronger and surer.

In the books in this series, Dr. Murphy has synthesized the profundities of this power and has put them into an easily understood and pragmatic form so that you can apply them immediately to your life. As Dr. Murphy was a Protestant minister, many of his examples and citations come from the Bible. The concepts these passages illustrate should not be viewed as sectarian. Indeed, their messages are universal and are preached in most religions and philosophies. He often reiterated that the essence of knowledge is in the law of life and belief. It is not Catholic, Protestant, Muslim, or Hindu; it is pure and simple faith: "Do unto others accordingly."

Dr. Murphy's wife, Dr. Jean Murphy, continued his ministry after his death in 1981. In a lecture she gave in 1986, quoting her late husband, she reiterated his philosophy:

> I want to teach men and women of their Divine Origin, and the powers pregnant within them. I want to inform them that this power is within and that they are their own saviors and capable of achieving their own salvation. This is the message of the Bible, and nine-tenths of our confusion today is due to wrongful, literal interpretation of the life-transforming truths offered in it.
>
> I want to reach the majority, the man on the street, the woman overburdened with duty and suppression of her talents and abilities. I want to help others at every stage or level of consciousness to learn of the wonders within.

She said of her husband: "He was a practical mystic, possessed by the intellect of a scholar, the mind of a successful executive, the heart of the poet." His message summed up was: "You are the king, the ruler of your world, for you are one with God."

Joseph Murphy was a firm believer that it was God's plan for people to be healthy, prosperous, and happy. He countered those theologians and others who claimed that desire is evil and urged people to crush it. He said that extinction of our longings means apathy—no feeling, no action. He preached that desire is a gift of God. It is healthy and wholesome to want to become more and better than we were yesterday . . . in the areas of health, abundance, companionship, security, and more. How could these be wrong?

Desire is behind all progress. Without it, nothing would be accomplished. It is the creative power and must be channeled constructively. For example, if one is poor, yearning for wealth wells up from within; if one is ill, there is a wish for health; if lonely, there is a desire for companionship and love.

We must believe that we can improve our lives. A belief—whether it is true, false, or merely indifferent—sustained over a period of time becomes assimilated and is incorporated into our mentality. Unless countermanded by faith of an opposite nature, sooner or later it takes form and is expressed or experienced as fact, form, condition, circumstance, and the events of life. We have the power within us to change negative beliefs to positive ones, and thereby change ourselves for the better.

You give the command and your subconscious mind will faithfully obey it. You will get a reaction or response according to the nature of the thought you hold in your conscious mind. Psychologists and psychiatrists point out that when thoughts are conveyed to your subconscious mind, impressions are made in your brain cells. As soon as this part of you accepts any idea, it proceeds to put it into effect immediately. It works by association of ideas and uses every bit of knowledge that you have gathered in your lifetime to bring about its purpose. It draws on the infinite power, energy, and wisdom within you, lining up all the laws of nature to get its way. Sometimes it seems to bring about an immediate solution to your difficulties, but at other times it may take days, weeks, or longer.

The habitual thinking of your conscious mind establishes deep grooves in your subconscious mind. This is very favorable for you if your recurring thoughts are harmonious, peaceful, and constructive. On the other hand, if you have indulged in fear, worry, and other destructive concepts, the remedy is to recognize the omnipotence of your subconscious and decree freedom, happiness, perfect health, and prosperity. Your subconscious mind, being creative and one with your Divine Source, will proceed to create the freedom and happiness that you have earnestly declared.

Now for the first time, Dr. Murphy's lectures have been combined, edited, and updated in six new books that bring his teachings into the 21st century. To enhance and augment this original text, we have incorporated material from some of Jean Murphy's lectures and have added examples of people whose success reflects Dr. Murphy's philosophy.

The other works in this series are listed on the second page of this book, but just reading them will not improve your state of being. To truly maximize your potential, you must study these principles, take them to heart, integrate them into your mentality, and apply them as an integral part of your approach to every aspect of your life.

— **Arthur R. Pell, Ph.D.**, editor

᚛✛᚜ ᚛✛᚜

Editor's Note: While updating these works, at times I have added current examples (that is, events and situations that may have occurred after Joseph Murphy's death) showing how basic principles presented by the author are still valid.

Preface

*S*elf-confidence, the feeling that you can accomplish anything you set out to do, is the essential element in living a full and meaningful life. The main reason many people never succeed in their jobs, business ventures, and even personal lives is a lack of this key ingredient. Why don't some individuals have self-confidence? One common reason is that they've failed in some activity early in their lives and fear that this will happen again. Another is that other people—often their own parents—were never satisfied with their performance in school or other areas and have left them with a feeling of inferiority. Still others have tasted achievement only to have it followed by some sort of failure, and they've let that setback dominate their minds and doom them to a void of self-confidence in anything they do.

Can this be changed? Of course it can. In this book, Dr. Joseph Murphy provides a surefire cure for a lack of self-confidence. It has worked for a multitude of his readers and listeners, and it will be effective for you.

Self-confidence is an integral part of self-esteem. Before you can gain confidence in the decisions you make, you must believe in yourself. You must truly feel that you're someone of worth. If you don't have self-esteem, how can you be assured that your choices are worthwhile?

Too often, we're more concerned about what others think of us than about how *we* view ourselves. William Boetcker, a 20th century clergyman and writer, admonished his readers: "Never mind what 'people' think of you. They may overestimate or underestimate you!

Until they discover your real worth, your success depends mainly upon what you think of yourself and whether you believe in yourself. You can succeed if nobody else believes it, but you will never succeed if you don't believe in yourself."

In the following pages, Dr. Murphy will show you how prayer can help you program your subconscious mind to overcome negative feelings about yourself and build or rebuild self-esteem—and with that, self-confidence.

You may say that you've tried prayer and it doesn't work for you. However, a lack of confidence and too much effort is the reason that you don't get an answer to your prayers. Many people sabotage themselves by failing to fully comprehend the workings of the subconscious mind. When you know how this functions, you gain a measure of confidence. You must remember that whenever your deeper mind accepts an idea, it immediately begins to execute it, mobilizing all its mighty resources to that end. This law is true for good or bad ideas; consequently, if you use it negatively, it brings trouble, failure, and confusion. If you use it constructively, it brings guidance, freedom, and peace of mind.

Wonderful results are inevitable when your thoughts are constructive, you're in tune with the Infinite, and you have love and goodwill for all. Therefore, it's perfectly obvious that the only thing you have to do in order to overcome obstacles is to get your subconscious to accept your idea or request by feeling its reality now. The law of your mind will do the rest. Give your prayer to God with faith and confidence, and your subconscious will take over and bring you the desired outcome.

You will always fail to get results if you use mental coercion or force, saying, "I tried so hard." Your subconscious mind doesn't respond to coercion: It responds to your faith or conscious acceptance of your good. Your failure to get what you want may also arise from making statements such as, "Things are getting worse"; "I'll never get an answer"; "I see no way out"; "It's hopeless"; "I don't know what to do"; or "I'm all mixed up." When you make such declarations, you get no response or cooperation from your subconscious mind. You're like a soldier marking time and you get nowhere.

Your subconscious is always controlled by the dominant idea you hold and will accept the stronger of two contradictory propositions. If you say, "I want self-confidence but can't get it; I try so hard, force myself to pray, and use all the willpower I have," you must realize that your error lies in your effort. Never try to compel the subconscious mind to accept your idea by exercising force and dogged determination. Such attempts are doomed to failure, and you'll get the opposite of what you pray for.

It's the quiet mind that gets things done. Your strength lies in being calm and confident—not in getting agitated and worked up about the conditions of the world. You can't change external circumstances, but you *can* transform yourself. You may disapprove of what people do, and it's certainly right to condemn mugging, rape, murder, and that sort of thing. You do the best you can: You write to your political leaders, participate in voting, and cooperate with police; but the most important thing is to have a tranquil mind. Keep it aligned with the Infinite Presence, because agitation, resentment, hatred, and anger solve no problems; they only make matters worse. You're pouring out more toxins and effluvia on the mass mind, and you're doing more harm than good.

If you're suffering from inner turmoil, you can't help anyone. If you have low self-esteem and lack confidence, you'll be a poor companion, parent, and co-worker. The degree of success that you can achieve is directly proportionate to your serenity, insight, and realization that there's an Infinite Intelligence within you that guides and directs you and reveals to you the perfect plan.

God is the Living Spirit Almighty within you. It's the only creative power there is, whether you call it *Jehovah, Allah, Brahma,* or something else. Your thought is creative. Therefore, if you focus on good, you will receive wonderful results; if you think about evil, evil will follow; if you dwell on lack, that's what you'll get; and if you keep your mind on God's riches, you'll enjoy prosperity. This law of mind is the only power you have, and it's God, too.

What governs you? It's *your* beliefs about yourself; the opinions of other don't matter. If someone says to you, "You're a failure; you'll never amount to anything," what should you do? Tell yourself, "I was born to win and I'm going to succeed in a remarkable and unique way. The power of the Almighty flows through me." Every time anyone tells you that you're going to be defeated, it's a stimulus for you to reinforce your faith in the Almighty Power, which never fails. In other words, you have to wake up and stop blaming people and conditions. You're responsible for your choices. Sure, there will be setbacks, but that doesn't mean that *you* are a failure. You have within you the creative power to reverse failure and move on to success. The other person doesn't control you or have the power to manipulate you unless you allow it.

Your self-confidence grows with each success you have and even when you meet the occasional defeat, because you know that the Creative Power of God is within you. You believe in it—and therefore in yourself.

You're what you think you are. You create yourself in the image you have of yourself in your own mind. Self-esteem and confidence are nothing more than the projection of your thoughts, and if you maintain a strong, positive view of yourself, you'll be a happier and more successful person. You'll be able to hurdle roadblocks—no matter how difficult—and achieve the goals you set for yourself.

— **Arthur R. Pell, Ph.D.,** editor

⊯✦⊯ ⊯✦⊯

Chapter One

Building Self-Confidence

*I*f you think of yourself as a failure, you will fail. Instead, think about success. Realize that you were born to win and the Infinite can't be defeated. Picture yourself as successful, happy, and free . . . and you will be. Whatever you think and feel with your conscious mind is embodied in your subconscious and comes to pass in your experience. That's the law of mind, and it's undeviating, immutable, and timeless.

We're not talking about having faith in dogmas, traditions, or any religious teachings; but about believing in the laws of your own mind and the goodness of God in the land of the living—that Creative Intelligence that responds to your thought. You can have a belief that you'll catch a cold when you're exposed to a draft or when somebody sneezes, and you can even have faith that your business ventures will fail. In these cases, you're focusing on the wrong thing and will reap negative results.

A woman once said to me, "For ten years, I had absolute faith that I would be alone in life, no one would marry me, and I would be poor and miserable. Then I read your book *The Power of Your Subconscious Mind* and applied the prayers it outlined. Now I'm happily married, have a marvelous husband, and have been blessed with three lovely children."

This woman reversed her faith in the negative to a joyous expectancy of the best in all aspects of her life. Fear is faith in the wrong thing. Instead, believe in the goodness of God, Divine

Love, and the Healing Presence. This woman's subconscious mind responded to her belief, for the law of life is the law of belief.

What do you believe in? To believe is to accept something as true. Trust in whatever is true, lovely, just, pure, and good. If something is worthy or has virtue, have faith in it.

Your greatest need is to believe in yourself, what you're doing, and your ultimate destiny. Self-confidence finds its greatest outlet when it's accompanied by a belief that your real self is God and that with God, all things are possible.

The Bible provides the key to building spiritual self-reliance, but without faith, it's impossible to please God. You must first believe that God *is* and that He rewards those who diligently seek Him. Down through the ages, all men and women who have possessed spiritual self-reliance have had a deep, abiding conviction that they were one with the God Presence within.

God is the Living Spirit within you and has no face, form, or figure; it's timeless, shapeless, and ageless. Give your attention, devotion, and loyalty to the Divine Love within you that created the universe and you. It's all-powerful, all-knowing, and all-seeing. When you're in tune with it, Infinite Power responds to you, and you do marvelous things.

Great people throughout history have had self-confidence without being overly aggressive, egotistical, or intolerant. Jesus, Moses, Buddha, Lao-Tzu, Confucius, Mohammed, and many others accomplished the so-called impossible through the absolute conviction that they could achieve what they desired by relying on the Divine Power that strengthened and inspired them. They were all human beings like you.

You can accomplish little in this world without faith. For example, when farmers plant seeds, they have faith in the laws of agriculture. Chemists have faith in the principles of chemistry; and medical professionals have faith in their knowledge of anatomy, physiology, and pharmacology, and surgery. Similarly, engineers have implicit faith in the rules of mathematics and physics. They construct buildings according to scientific laws that existed before any humans walked this earth and any church was formed.

You can have the same abiding faith in the laws of your own mind, which are the same yesterday, today, and forever.

Anyone who thinks that the axioms of chemistry, physics, and mathematics are different from the laws operating in the mind is living in the Dark Ages. These mental and spiritual laws are just as dependable and undeviating as the principle of gravity. We know for a fact that if you think about good, positive results will unfold; and that if you think about evil, negative results will follow.

The first step in building self-confidence is to believe in that Infinite Power within you that grows your hair and nails and digests your food. It watches over you when you're asleep and governs your heartbeat and all the vital organs and processes of your body. For example, if you cut yourself, it heals you without any effort on your part. If you get burned, the Healing Presence reduces the edema and gives you new tissue and skin. The Life Principle within you always seeks to heal you. You also know that you're alive and have a mind and spirit because you can feel joy, rapture, and love when you look into your child's eyes. All these emotions are invisible, yet they're real.

Therefore, believe in that Infinite Power within you. Recognize and know that your essence is God. The Living Spirit within you was never born and will never die. It's the very Life Principle in you, through you, and all around you.

The second step is to commune regularly with this Almighty Presence. Create a vision, realizing that your reality will conform to this powerful image. Your vision is what you're giving attention to and what you're silently thinking at this very moment. That's where you're going, and that's what's going to happen to you. Let your dream be about abundance, right action, inspiration, and Divine Love; and you'll become like the snow on the mountain that's melted by the heat of the sun and flows downward like a river of life, giving nourishment and sustenance to the valleys.

What difference does it make if you've floundered and failed many times? *Now* you know that the Divine Presence dwells within you, responds to you, and wants you to be happy. Stir up that Infinite Spirit within you and awaken that sleeping giant within. Trust that Creative Intelligence within you even more than you ever trusted your human father or mother.

When the thought *I can't do this* comes to you, mentally affirm: *But the Divine Presence can. It's infinitely powerful and nothing can oppose or challenge it. It's all-mighty.* If negative thoughts arise, look at all the difficulties and obstructions and say to yourself boldly: "Infinite Intelligence and Power knows no obstacles, delays, or impediments." Find an affirmation that counteracts all your pessimistic thoughts, and your life will become more blessed and beautiful through the years. You'll find that your obstructions and challenges will be transformed into opportunities. Your fear will turn to faith, and your doubt will be transformed into certainty that the All-Knowing Presence is within you and that wonders unfold as you tune in to It.

I had an intensely interesting conversation with a hotel proprietor in Lisbon, Portugal. He told me that he'd started out as a waiter in a small restaurant. When the boss would ask him to do something special, he'd often say, "I'm going to try to do it." His employer finally told him, "Never say 'I'm going to *try*' . . . say, 'I'm going to *do* it,' and know that you can. Then God will respond to you." The hotel owner continued, "I profited from that advice and never again said, 'I'm going to try.' I began to believe in myself and know that the Infinite Presence dwells within me."

This man began to affirm, perhaps a thousand times a day: "I'm going to own a big hotel." He believed that through the Power of the Infinite, he would do exactly that. One day he felt an overwhelming urge to go to the casinos in Monaco, and he asked a friend to accompany him and show him the ropes. He knew that he'd win—it was an inner, silent knowing of the soul. He had fabulous winnings playing roulette, and when he had enough money ($100,000) for a deposit on his hotel, he stopped and never gambled again. This was the way his subconscious mind answered his prayer. He told me, "I opened this hotel and have now paid off the mortgage. I've prospered beyond my fondest dreams."

Make up your mind now—this minute—that you *can* achieve what you desire, be what you sincerely wish to be, and have what you want to possess; and it will be done unto you as you believe. Let nothing stop you or shake your conviction, for with this kind of belief, you will inevitably succeed and move forward in life.

What does an immensely wealthy person or a prominent business executive possess that you do not? Only one thing: self-confidence. They believe in themselves and the power within them. Confidence means faith in a principle and the powers of your mind. The first step in building this assurance is to believe in that Infinite Power within you. Successful people put their trust in the Guiding Principle or Divine Love and as a result, radiate power and confidence. They therefore win your respect the first time you meet them.

Last year I interviewed an extremely wealthy man in Hilo, Hawaii. He said to me sadly, "I'm nobody and no one cares for me." Frankly, no one did—for the simple reason that he didn't respect or love himself and was self-critical even though he had vast real estate holdings and large bank accounts.

If you're cruel or mean to yourself, others will also be harsh with you . . . for as within, so without. I explained to him that because he was constantly criticizing and belittling himself, others were treating him the same way. I also told him that if he didn't expect people to treat him well, they wouldn't.

I pointed out to him that the riches of the Infinite were within him and all around him. As Shakespeare said, "All things are ready, if our minds be so." All he had to do was call on the Divine Presence and Power, and it would respond to his thought. He began to use some of the great eternal truths of the Bible, which I outlined for him as follows:

> *Know ye not that ye are the temple of the Living God and that the Spirit of God dwelleth in you? But the fruit of the Spirit is love, joy, peace, patience, gentleness, goodness, faith, meekness, and temperance. Ye wilt be kept in perfect peace because*

ye trusteth in Him. In all thy ways acknowledge Him, and He
shall make plain thy path. Believe in Him, and He shall bring it
to pass.

Rejoice and be glad that the Infinite Being created you. Know
that Infinite Spirit is always with you and is capable of healing,
restoring, and energizing you. All things work together for the
good of those who love God, and the Divine Essence within you is
healing you now.

In a Nutshell

If you think of yourself as a failure, you will fail. Instead, think
about success and realize that you were born to succeed, for the
Infinite can't be defeated. Picture yourself as successful, happy,
and free . . . and you will be. Whatever you think and feel is true
in your conscious mind is embodied in your subconscious and
comes to pass in your experience. That's the law of mind; and it's
undeviating, immutable, and timeless.

Your greatest need is to believe in yourself, what you're doing,
and your ultimate destiny. Self-reliance or self-confidence finds its
greatest outlet when it's accompanied by a belief that your real self
is God, and that with God, all things are possible.

The first step in building self-confidence is to believe in that
Infinite Power within you.

What do immensely wealthy people or prominent business
executives possess that you do not? Only one thing: self-confidence.
They believe in themselves and the power within them. Confidence
means faith in a principle and the powers of your mind.

Make up your mind now—this minute—that you *can* achieve
what you desire, become what you sincerely wish to be, and have what
you want to possess; and it will be done unto you as you believe.

᪥✝᪥   ᪥✝᪥

Chapter Two

---••••---

Learning to Love Yourself

One of the most profound and deep-seated longings of the heart is to be respected, loved, and esteemed. In the Bible, you're told to "love your neighbor as yourself." And Carlyle said, "In this world there is one godlike thing, the essence of all that was or ever will be of godlike in this world: the veneration done to Human Worth by the hearts of men." However, you can't truly care for others unless you love yourself.

In the beautiful 8th Psalm, David writes eloquently of the tremendous potential of humankind:

> *When I consider your heavens, the work of Your fingers,*
> *The moon and the stars, which You have ordained,*
> *What is man that You are mindful of him,*
> *And the son of man that You visit him?*
> *For You have made him a little lower than the angels,*
> *And You have crowned him with glory and honor.*

Today we're witnessing the work of Infinite Intelligence in our countless new discoveries. We're living in an age of supersonic speed, computing innovation, and atomic power. All of these miracles of air, space, and sea came out of the human mind.

We're also penetrating and navigating the mysteries of the deeper mind and are gradually becoming aware of the kingdom of God within us. Research work at Duke University and other academic laboratories is revealing the powers of the subconscious and such phenomena as telepathy, clairvoyance, clairaudience, telekinesis, astral travel, and precognition

౼✛౽

I received a letter from a woman in Arizona who wrote that her sister-in-law and mother-in-law disapproved of her and had told her bluntly that they preferred her husband's former wife. They never invited her to their homes and always asked her husband to visit them without her. Furthermore, although she tried her best to be nice to them, they criticized her meals, home, clothing, and speech. This woman stated that she felt inferior and rejected, and she asked me, "Why do they do this? What's wrong with me?"

In reply, I pointed out that she'd been suffering unnecessarily and that she had the power to reject the poisonous statements and rudeness of her in-laws. I explained further that she didn't create her relatives and that she wasn't responsible for their jealous attitudes and neurotic complexes.

I told her to stop being a doormat for them and allowing them to step on her. I added that it was quite possible that her charm, graciousness, kindness, and wonderful character annoyed them and that they derived sadistic satisfaction from disturbing her.

I also suggested that she break off all relations with her in-laws and focus on developing esteem for herself. In other words, she needed to love herself and become aware that her true essence is God. I gave her the following prayer:

> *I completely surrender my in-laws to God. He created and sustains them. I radiate love, peace, and goodwill to them; and I wish for them all the blessings of heaven. I'm a child of the Divine, Who loves and cares for me. When a negative thought of anger, fear, self-condemnation, or resentment enters my mind, I immediately supplant it with the thought of God within me. I know I have complete dominion over my thoughts and emotions*

because I'm part of Infinite Spirit. I now think along harmonious, constructive lines. Only the ideas of the Infinite Presence enter my mind, bringing me harmony, health, and peace. Whenever I start to demean myself, I will stop and boldly affirm: "I exalt the Divine in the midst of me. I'm one with God—and one with God is a majority. If the All-Powerful Spirit is for me, who can be against me?"

This woman experienced a complete transformation of her mind and heart as she repeated this prayer many times every day. She told me, "This process has worked wonders for me. My husband said to me the other day, 'You're beaming! What happened to you?'"

⊰✦⊱

A few years ago, I had a consultation with a salesman who said that he was timid and resentful and saw the world as harsh and cruel. He also told me that his wife, boss, and associates didn't appreciate him and that even his children looked down on him. He asked me, "How can I gain the respect and appreciation of others?"

I explained to him that *he* needed to develop a sense of self-appreciation and love himself. I stated, "If you despise and belittle yourself, you can't have esteem and goodwill for others, for it's a cosmic law of mind that we're constantly projecting our thoughts, feelings, and beliefs onto others. And what we send out comes back to us. The cause of all of your problems is your feelings of insecurity and inadequacy.

"We're all children of the Infinite, and every quality and power of God is within us, waiting to be expressed. You should certainly love, honor, and exalt the Divine Presence within you. It has nothing at all to do with egoism, self-aggrandizement, narcissism, or anything of that nature. On the contrary, it's a wholesome veneration of the Divinity within you, for you're a temple of the Powerful Presence. Supreme Intelligence created, animates, and sustains you. Give your allegiance to It instead of to conditions, circumstances, stars, men, women, or any material object. The moment you devote yourself to these external things, you cease to love or be loyal to God.

"The Sovereign Spirit within creates everything. Therefore, wise people don't put their faith in the phenomenalistic world; instead, they give their power to the Divine Creative Power within them. By honoring and venerating God, you also love yourself—and you'll automatically respect the Divinity in others. But if you don't cherish your holy inner essence, you can't love your wife, friends, or anybody else because you can't give what you don't have.

"As Emerson says: 'I, the imperfect, adore the Perfect.' Glorify God in your body, for you're a child of the Divine. When you honor, respect, and love your true self, you will automatically do the same for others."

The salesman listened carefully, then said to me, "I've never heard it explained that way before. I can see clearly now what I've been doing. I've been down on myself and full of prejudices, ill will, and bitterness. And what I've been sending out has reverberated back to me. I've gained true insight into myself."

He began to affirm the following truths with deep sincerity several times a day, knowing that they would sink from his conscious mind into his subconscious and blossom like seeds:

> *I know that I can give only what I have. From this moment forward, I'm going to have a wholesome and deep respect for my real self, which is God. I'm an expression of the Divine One, Who needs me to be where I am; otherwise, I wouldn't be here. From this moment forward, I honor and salute the Holy Presence in all of my associates and in all people everywhere. I hold the soul of every person in veneration and esteem. I'm one with the Infinite and am a tremendous success. And I wish for everyone what I desire for myself. I'm at peace.*

This young man has transformed his life. He's no longer shy or angry or constantly apologizing for being alive. He's grown by leaps and bounds—and so can you. If you learn to love your true self, you'll know how to treasure and respect others. If you put yourself down or are mean to yourself, you can't think well of others because you project your opinions and mood onto them.

Yes, learn to cherish yourself and understand the true meaning of love. The self is the Divinity within. Give your allegiance and devotion to this Infinite Presence, and refuse to give power to any external thing. I want to emphasize this because if you're worshiping stars, suns, moons, or anything like that, you've wandered away from the Divine.

⌖

There's a type of mother who neglects herself. She wears old clothes, eats cheap food, and gives the best to her children. She survives on doughnuts and gives *them* filet mignon. I suppose she thinks her behavior is noble, but it's actually a very poor example for her kids. She should have the most beautiful wardrobe, dine on the most gourmet dishes, and teach her children about the riches of the Infinite. She needs to love herself in order to honor the Divine in them. They're all aspects of the Eternal Presence.

⌖

I received a letter from a man who stated that he couldn't understand why everybody around him annoyed him. I asked him to come see me, and I discovered that *he* was constantly irritating other people. He didn't like himself and was full of self-condemnation. Self-criticism is the most destructive mental poison. It seeps into your system and robs you of vitality, enthusiasm, and energy, leaving you a physical and mental wreck.

This man spoke in a tense tone that grated on one's nerves. He thought mainly about himself and was highly critical of others. I explained to him that while his unhappy experiences seemed to be about other people, his relationship with them was determined by his thoughts and feelings about *himself.* If he despised himself, he couldn't have goodwill and respect for others.

He began to realize that as long as he projected feelings of prejudice, ill will, and contempt for others, that's exactly what he would get back, because his world was but an echo of his moods and attitudes. I therefore gave him an affirmation that enabled him to overcome his irritation and arrogance. He decided to focus on inscribing the following thoughts in his subconscious mind:

> *I practice the golden rule from now on, which means that I think, speak, and act toward others as I wish them to think, speak, and act toward me. I sincerely desire peace, prosperity, and success for everyone. I'm always poised, serene, and calm. The peace of God floods my mind and whole being. Others appreciate and respect me as I appreciate myself. Life is honoring me greatly and provides for me abundantly. The petty things no longer irritate me. When fear, worry, doubt, or criticism knock at the door of my mind, my faith in goodness, truth, and beauty respond and find no one there. The suggestions and statements of others have no power to disturb me; the only force is the movement of my own thought. When I focus on positive ideas, the Divine Spirit supports me.*

He affirmed these truths morning and night and committed the whole prayer to memory. He put his emotion and love into these words, and they gradually penetrated the layers of his subconscious. A few weeks later, he said, "I know full well that my new understanding of my mind and how it works has changed my entire life. I'm getting along fine with others, and I received two promotions in the past two months. I now know the truth of the biblical passage: 'And I, if I be lifted up from the earth, will draw all men unto me.'"

This young man learned that the trouble was within himself; and he decided to change his thoughts, feelings, and reactions.

Anyone can do the same. It takes a decision, stick-to-itiveness, and a keen desire to transform oneself.

※✦※

An astronomer friend of mine recently told me that for years he'd scanned the heavens seeking to understand the story of creation and the riddle of the universe through his telescope. However, he said that lately he's been looking within himself—the person at the small end of the telescope—for understanding. He added that the answers to the mystery of the cosmos is within *us,* because the Infinite Spirit is our essence. When we understand ourselves, we will understand the universe.

Now is the time for us to analyze the analyzer. In trying to find happiness, peace, and prosperity outside of ourselves, we've neglected to look within to the unlimited storehouse of riches in our subconscious mind. Where else can we find balance, peace, and happiness but in our own mind?

Always exalt the Eternal Presence in you. Whenever you catch yourself being self-critical, stop and say: "I honor the Divine within that heals me." If you need to repeat this a thousand times a day, do so. After a while, you'll begin to do it automatically, and you'll love yourself more and more.

William Shakespeare said: "What a piece of work is a man! How noble in reason! how infinite in faculty! in form and moving how express and admirable! in action how like an angel! in understanding how like a god! the beauty of the world! the paragon of animals!" After you read that beautiful passage, do you have a new estimate of yourself? Can you develop a respect for that Divine Presence within that started your heartbeat and watches over you when you're asleep?

Emerson wrote: "There is one mind common to all individual men. Every man is an inlet to the same and to all of the same." Begin to realize that Infinite Intelligence—the Guiding Principle of the universe—is within you. It's your Higher Self. I'm not talking about your ego or your intellect, but about the inner Eternal Being that heals a cut on your finger and governs all your vital organs and functions of your body. You have the capacity to make choices and use your imagination and all of the other powers of God within you. There's only one Infinite Power, and you can tap into It.

When you consciously, decisively, and constructively use the Infinite Wisdom within you, you become free. As Emerson stated: "He that is once admitted to the right of reason is a freeman of the whole estate." Emerson was America's greatest philosopher and one of the most profound thinkers of all times. He was constantly in tune with the Infinite, and he urged everyone to release the unlimited potential within. He also taught about the dignity and grandeur of humankind and pointed out that we're all capable of greatness. He wrote: "What Plato has thought, he [every person] may think; what a saint has felt, he may feel; what at any time has befallen any man, he may understand. He who has access to the universal mind is a party to all that is or can be done, for this is the only and sovereign agent."

⊶✦⊷

A lady wrote to me: "My husband left me a year ago for a younger woman. I suffered from intense rage and hatred that my doctor said caused my sudden development of arthritis. Every day for the past three months, I have boldly affirmed—as you suggested—that my body is a temple of the Living God and that I glorify the Divine in my physical self. Every morning, afternoon, and evening, I declare that God's love permeates every atom of my being. I also prayed for my ex-husband. I knew in my heart that when God's love came into my soul, all the hate would drain out of me. Love casts out hate, peace casts out pain, and joy casts out sadness.

"There has been a remarkable change in my body. The excruciating pain has subsided, my joints have become more supple and mobile, and the calcareous deposits are gradually disappearing. My doctor is delighted—and so am I. I continue to realize that I'm a child of God and that He loves and cares for me. I know that this new self-appraisal has brought wonders into my life. All of my hatred of my ex-husband has evaporated, and I'm on the way to perfect health. Divine law and order govern me."

This woman discovered that when she began to honor, exalt, and call upon the Divine Presence within, It responded with the emotions of love, peace, harmony, confidence, joy, vitality, wholeness, and goodwill. As she started to love and respect herself, she found that all hatred vanished, and love rushed in to fill the vacuum.

You can glorify the God within as well. Open your mind and heart right now. Let in the influx of the Holy Spirit and realize that Its river of peace flows through you. Feel the infinite ocean of Divine Love saturate your whole being. You're bathed by the light and are immersed in the Omnipresence. Continue to realize that you're a child of the Living God, and wonders will happen in your life, too.

Love is the fulfillment of the law of health, happiness, success, and prosperity. According to the law of mind, you become what you contemplate, and what you really feel and believe deep down in your heart will always be made manifest.

Believe in the goodness of Infinite Spirit in the land of the living. To worship is to give your supreme adoration and veneration to that Higher Self in you—to count It worthy of the greatest attention and devotion and refuse to give power to any external thing, man, woman, or child. Know that the God in the other is the same God in you; therefore, if you hurt someone else, you're hurting yourself. That would be foolish.

Knowing this, practice a magnificent affirmation. Say to yourself: "I bless and exalt God in the midst of me, and I honor and venerate God in others." If you're married, salute the Divinity in your wife or husband. Claim that what's true of the Infinite Spirit is true of him or her, and the marriage will grow more wonderful through the years.

Psychologists tell us that each of us creates a "script" for our life. We might develop a story that's about high self-esteem and optimism and makes us happy—or one about self-doubt and pessimism that troubles us. Please don't interpret this to mean that people with lots of self-confidence are always cheerful and positive, while those with low self-esteem are always depressed. We all go through difficult, trying times. The difference is that those with a positive script bounce back more easily than those with a negative one.

Is it important to like yourself? Of course it is! God created humankind in His image and commanded that we love the Lord with all our might, strength, and being. Therefore, having a high sense of self-worth is essential if we're to honor God.

Many people who have had low opinions of themselves have been able to overcome this by taking steps to enhance their self-confidence. Unfortunately, low self-esteem—or worse, self-loathing—may have deep psychological roots. In such cases, professional assistance is needed to overcome it. However, most of us don't actually hate ourselves. We may just have temporary slumps in our confidence that we need to address. If these setbacks aren't dealt with, they may lead to more serious consequences. We don't need a psychologist for this; we can do it ourselves. Encouragement from a friend, spouse, pastor, or boss is helpful; but even without such a support person, we can rewrite the scripts on which we base our lives.

All of us have had both successes and failures in our lives. There are two consequences of failure: the tangible aspects or the problem itself, and the intangible—the depression and loss of self-esteem that accompanies a defeat or disappointment. We can take practical measures to handle the tangible problems, but coping with the psychological aspects is more complex. However, it can and must be done; otherwise, we fall into depression, become self-loathing, and doom ourselves to misery and continued failure.

We can overcome this downward spiral by concentrating on our achievements and successes. When we feel blue and our self-esteem is at a low ebb, we can reflect on our past accomplishments instead of dwelling on our mistakes. We've succeeded before and we can do it again. This reinforces our self-confidence and enables us to change the script in our minds.

Self-esteem is perishable and must constantly be nourished and reinforced. Just as the athletes on a team sometimes need a pep talk from their coach, we also need to hear encouraging words that boost our energy and self-confidence when our enthusiasm wanes or we suffer setbacks. But who's our coach? One of our principal mentors is ourselves. We can give ourselves inspirational talks and encouragement. To change the scripts in our minds, we must remind ourselves that we're good, we're winners, and we will succeed.

We also have a higher-level coach: God. We invite the Infinite Presence to guide and help us overcome depression and pessimism through prayer. We ask God to suffuse our spirits and let His will prevail in our lives. Prayer cannot bring water to parched fields, mend a broken bridge, or rebuild a ruined city; but it can water an arid soul, mend a shattered heart, and rebuild a weakened will.

Our self-esteem governs our lives. In our youth, it pushes us forward; in our middle years, it sustains us; and in our later years, it renews us. We must replace the negative words in our personal scripts with positive ones. Instead of making statements of despair, failure, hate, worry, and apathy, make proclamations of hope, victory, encouragement, enthusiasm, and love. We need to feed our minds and souls with prayers of joy, renewal, and strength.

In a Nutshell

Your real essence is God. When you honor and exalt the Infinite Presence within, you will automatically respect the Divinity in others. But if you don't love yourself, you can't cherish your wife, husband, or anybody else . . . because you can't give what you don't have.

If you despise yourself, you can't have goodwill and respect for others. It's a law of mind that we're always projecting our thoughts and feelings onto our associates and all of those around us.

In trying to find happiness, peace, and prosperity outside of ourselves, we've neglected to look within to the unlimited storehouse of riches of our subconscious. Where else will you find abundance, joy, and ease but in your own mind?

Is it important to like yourself? Of course it is! God created humankind in His image and commanded that we love the Lord with all our might, strength, and being. Therefore, having a great sense of self-worth is essential if we're to honor and respect God.

When we feel depressed and our self-esteem is at a low ebb, we need to reflect on our past accomplishments instead of sulking. We've succeeded before and we can do it again. This reinforces our self-confidence and changes the script in our minds from a tale of defeat to a story of triumph.

We need to feed our minds and souls with prayers of encouragement, love, and prosperity.

✠ ✠

Chapter Three

---•◦•---

Love and a New Self-Image

*T*he word *image* is related to the term *imagination*, which is the workshop of God. Imagination clothes all ideas and gives them form. Using the power of your mind, you can bring the images of your dreams into reality as that which is hidden in your subconscious is made manifest.

Let's take some examples. When you were preparing for your wedding, you probably had a vivid picture of what you wanted in your mind. You heard the music and vows, saw the church and flowers, and envisioned the ring on your finger. You traveled in your imagination on your honeymoon to Europe, Niagara Falls, or some other exotic location. Similarly, when you were in school, you may have imagined what your graduation would be like. A beautiful drama took place in your mind. You saw the president of the college giving you your diploma and visualized all the students dressed in caps and gowns. You heard your mother, father, and friends congratulate you. You felt the hugs and kisses. It was all real, exciting, and wonderful.

Images appear freely in your mind as if from nowhere. But you know that there was and is an Internal Creator that manifests these visions. This Infinite Power can also help you develop a new self-image. Do you want to be greater, nobler, or more godlike than you now are? Well, you must give up fear, grudges, peeves, and self-condemnation. You must let go of negative thoughts in order to practice constructive thinking. Are you willing to release the old so that you might experience the new? What do you want to be? Imagine that you're now doing what you long to do.

A young woman who attended one of my talks recently wanted to be an actress. She was a wonderful dancer and singer and vividly imagined that she was performing onstage. She visualized the audience and heard her mother and friends congratulating her on a marvelous show. She felt the embrace of her mom. She played out the role in her mind over and over again—and it paid off. A few months later, she got a wonderful contract to perform in Las Vegas. Since then, she's also appeared in Reno. The woman developed a new image of herself and fell in love with it. She became entranced and fascinated with her dream, and it became a reality.

You can fall in love with music, art, or the law. You can sit down and contemplate health, happiness, peace of mind, abundance, security, right action, harmony, inspiration, and guidance. If you become fascinated and engrossed in an idea or desire, the law of your subconscious will respond. As you think in your heart and deeper mind, so you are. As you act, so you will become.

What you think in your head isn't as important as what you put in your heart because ideas have to be "emotionalized" and felt as true in order to be manifested. Any thought that you dwell upon induces and evokes a certain response and emotion. As you continue to focus, the idea sinks into your subconscious, impregnates it, and is expressed as form. You're compelled to be, do, and express that which you meditate on. That's the law of your deeper mind. All of your worries and concerns disappear as you fall in love with a higher image of yourself. You can now begin to think about these great truths.

The biographers of English poet John Keats say that he used his imagination wisely when he was confronted with difficulties and predicaments. If he was worried about anything, he would imagine himself sitting and talking with one of his friends and receiving the perfect advice and guidance about his situation. He would visualize the entire scene as vividly as possible, hearing the tone of the voices and seeing the gestures. He would receive the help he sought, for imagination is indeed the workshop of God.

On the other hand, some people use the imagination in a destructive way. For example, a businessman may be prospering but is dwelling on negativity. He runs a motion picture of failure in his mind, seeing the shelves of his store as empty, imagining himself going into bankruptcy, and visualizing his business having to be closed down. There's no truth whatsoever in his pessimistic mental images, for the things he fears don't exist—except in his morbid imagination. If he constantly indulges in these gloomy thoughts and charges them with energy, he will, of course, bring about his own failure. He has a choice between success or defeat, but he's choosing the latter.

Using the science of imagination, you can eliminate all the mental impurities, including fear, worry, and destructive self-talk. To do this, you must completely focus on your ideal. Just as the young woman I described earlier put all her attention on being a great dancer and singer, you must refuse to swerve from your purpose or aim in life. As you become mentally absorbed in your dream, you fall in love with a higher image of yourself, and you *will* see your desire take form in your world.

In the book of Joshua, it says: "Choose this day whom you will serve." Decide that you will serve Infinite Spirit. Imagine whatever is lovely, noble, and wonderful—and whatever gives you greater peace, health, vitality, and wealth.

=✧=

Your subconscious magnifies and multiplies whatever you give your attention to. As you continue to focus on something, you're compelled to do it. Therefore, don't try to overcome alcoholism or any other bad habit through willpower. All you're doing is mentally dwelling on the alcohol or other compulsion and setting the law of reversed effort into effect. You're actually driving yourself to drink because you're thinking about alcohol, looking at the glass, and filling your mind with thoughts of alcoholism. But if you instead focus your attention on peace of mind, sobriety, and divinity— realizing that the Almighty Power supports you—you will overcome your addiction.

I knew an attorney in New York who was an alcoholic and ended up in the gutter. He became a panhandler. He sincerely wanted to get sober and, at my suggestion, imagined that he was back at work, wearing a wonderful suit, and pleading the case of a client before a judge. He was running a motion picture in his own mind. He said, "That's what I want to be—back in the role of an attorney helping people and giving them advice." When he felt the temptation to drink, he flashed the movie through his mind. He did this again and again, and it naturally sank into his subconscious. His deeper mind took over and compelled him toward sobriety and inner peace.

We're not talking about daydreaming or idle fancy here. You must have confidence in what you're doing and why you're doing it, and then you will get results. In spite of the way you feel, imagine yourself being what you want to be. Insist on a magnificent performance even if you think you're a failure. Discipline your mind even when you may not feel like it. Let go of the negative imagery and instead direct your imagination and attention to what you want to be—and you will become it. Do it over and over again, practicing as you did when you learned to walk, play golf, or swim. Your subconscious assimilates the imagined pattern, and it becomes second nature. Continue your visualizations until your desired result becomes a living part of you. If you look at a mountain and repeatedly see yourself climbing to the top, you eventually will succeed because the deeper mind automatically responds to whatever you're feeding it.

⊨✛⊨

A few years ago, I flew to Reno at the request of a couple who'd been married for 20 years and were now contemplating divorce. While talking to them, I found that the wife was in the habit of belittling her husband. She admitted that she frequently screamed obscenities at him in restaurants and at private social gatherings. He complained that she constantly accused him of infidelities— which only took place in her imagination.

This woman suffered from extreme outbursts of temper and was intensely jealous. She also refused to admit that she was in any way responsible for the marital conflict. The husband was passive, quiet, and completely subservient to her moods. Of course, you're undoubtedly coming to the conclusion that someone who puts up with this sort of behavior is also sick. Yes, he was emotionally unhealthy and was acting like a doormat. He'd also developed ulcers and high blood pressure and suffered from suppressed rage.

The wife said that she'd come from a home where her mother was dominant, bossed her father around, and constantly cheated on him. She elaborated, "My mom had no morals and was cruel. My dad was a fool. He was easygoing, blind to what was going on, and completely subservient to her."

I explained to her why she was acting the way she was. First, she'd received no love or real affection as a child. Her mother had probably been jealous of her, making her feel inferior and unwanted. The wife's tyrannical behavior stemmed from a sense of fear, insecurity, and weakness. I also pointed out that her basic problem was that she refused to give love and goodwill to her husband and others.

Love was missing in their married life—and where there's no affection, there's nothing. Without kindness, consideration, compassion, and understanding, a marriage is an absolute farce.

At my suggestion, both of them began to look inward. She suddenly realized that she'd unconsciously married a man who allowed himself to be manipulated, henpecked, and emasculated. She also saw that her possessiveness, intense jealousy, and antagonism toward her husband were in reality a craving for the love she'd missed in childhood. However, he wasn't able to give her what she needed because he resented her so deeply. He said, "I've reached my limit. My doctor says, 'Get out!' Her constant nagging is making me sick, and life is unbearable."

The couple did finally agree that they wanted to make a go of the marriage, which required that both of them make an effort to change. The first step was for her to decide to stop doing and saying all the things that hurt and humiliated her husband. He, in turn, agreed to assert his rights, prerogatives, and privileges as a man and husband. He was no longer to be mousy and subservient to her tantrums and abusive language.

I gave the wife a simple prayer and asked her to do what's called a *mirror treatment.* (You can practice it, too.) She agreed to stand before the mirror in her bedroom three times a day—regularly and systematically—and boldly affirm the following:

> *I am a child of God. The Divine Presence loves and cares for me. I radiate warmth, peace, and goodwill to my husband. Every time I think about him, I affirm, "I love you and I care for you. I am happy, joyous, affectionate, kind, and harmonious; and I exude more and more of God's love every day."*

She committed this prayer to memory, which isn't hard to do. As she repeated it, she knew that these truths would be fulfilled, for the mind is a mirror that reflects back what is held before it. Her perseverance and stick-to-itiveness paid off, and at the end of two months she came to visit me in Beverly Hills. I saw a transformed woman who was kind, gentle, and bubbling over with new life. Yes, she had a new self-image and had fallen in love with this transformed view of herself.

Her husband's spiritual prescription was to stand before the mirror twice a day for about five minutes and make this affirmation:

> *I am strong, powerful, loving, harmonious, illumined, and inspired. I am a tremendous success and am happy and prosperous. I love my wife, and she loves me. Whenever I think of her, I say, "I love you and care for you."*

He realized as he affirmed these truths about himself that even though he might at first think he was a hypocrite to say these words, they would gradually sink into his subconscious mind and manifest—which they did. Both the husband and the wife were compelled to express what they'd impressed on their deeper mind, for that is the law. Now there's harmony where before there was discord, peace where there was pain, and love where there was hate.

It's impossible for you to stand before a mirror and make affirmations without getting results because you're engraving these thoughts in your subconscious. You're impregnating your deeper mind with these truths through repetition, faith, and expectancy. Just as it's the nature of an apple seed to become an apple tree, it's the nature of your thoughts to blossom as form.

You're here to stand up for your rights, privileges, and prerogatives. You're here to say yes to life and to all of the ideas that heal, bless, inspire, and elevate. Say no to anything that's false and to anyone who wants to drag you down. Absolutely refuse to accept lies.

❧✚❧

I talked to a troubled young man whose aunt brought him to visit me. It became obvious that he'd had an overbearing mother who gave him no love or understanding. As far back as he could remember, she'd exacted his obedience by whipping, criticizing, and condemning him.

He was now 18 and said that he had great difficulty getting along with anyone. His aunt had taken him into her loving, harmonious home, and he seemed to feel jealous of his cousins for having such affectionate parents. I explained to him that his present attitude was simply a defense mechanism that caused him to reject people who were kind and friendly and that his problem was due to the traumatic experiences of his childhood. His dad had deserted his mom when he was a baby and never visited or contacted his son.

The young man began to understand that his mother undoubtedly hated herself, because you must first hate yourself before you can reject anybody else. She was projecting that animosity toward her ex-husband, son, and all those close to her. I explained that the cure for him was simple and that all he had to do was change his image of his mom, because this was also the view he had of himself.

He used this technique: He pictured his mother in his mind's eye as happy, joyous, peaceful, and loving. He imagined her smiling and hugging him, saying, "I love you and am happy you came back." He could feel the warmth of the embrace and the kiss on his cheek. He vividly experienced this reunion in his mind. After six weeks, I heard from him again. He's back living with his mom and has been given a wonderful position with an electronics firm. He supplanted the destructive, hateful image of his mother with a positive, loving one, and he also transformed his own view of *himself.* It changed his life. Divine love entered into his heart and dissolved everything unlike itself.

⊰✦⊱

Love is the spirit of God. It's like the fire that gives out its heat to all corners of the room. It neither comes nor goes but fills all space. It's an outreaching of the heart and goodwill to all. When you love people, you want to see them become and express all that they long for. You exalt God in the midst of them. If a husband loves his wife, he wants her to express herself and release her talents to the world. He doesn't say, "You're married now so you must stay home and work in the kitchen." That kind of statement is the opposite of love, which always wishes freedom for everyone and allows people to do the seemingly impossible.

For instance, I recently read a magazine article about a 110-pound woman who lifted a 1,500-pound car to save her father's life. Robert Stone of Covina, California, was making repairs on his vehicle when the jack slipped and it fell on him. His 20-year-old daughter, Janet, heard his cries and found him pinned under the massive weight. In an incredible surge of strength, she lifted the car, freed her dad, carried him to her own automobile, and drove him to the hospital. This young daughter's love for her father and her intense desire to save his life seized her mind and caused the Power of the Almighty to respond to her focal point of attention, enabling her to perform the Herculean task that rescued him.

Remember that all of the strength of the Infinite is within you, enabling you to do extraordinary things in every area of life. It's the Intelligence of the All-Wise One that made you from a cell. It created the universe and everything in it. It governs the galaxies in space, causes the planets to move in their orbits, and makes the Earth turn on its axis. All is in Divine order, which is heaven's first law.

⚜

An outstanding singer in one of the casinos in Las Vegas told me that for several years he'd been a waiter but had always had an intense desire to sing. Many of his friends told him that he had all the qualities and abilities necessary to become a great performer. Then a customer in the restaurant where he worked gave him my book *The Power of Your Subconscious Mind*. He eagerly read it and practiced the techniques outlined in its pages every night.

He sat quietly for about ten minutes each evening and imagined that he was onstage singing to a wonderful audience. He made this mental image vivid and realistic. He visualized the people applauding him and praising his voice. He saw them smiling and experienced the warmth of their imaginary handshakes. At the end of about three weeks, he was offered a job as a singer. He experienced in reality what he'd pictured in his subconscious mind and realized the cherished desire of his heart.

⚜

A few years ago I visited a businessman in the hospital. He was very ill with shingles, which caused him great pain. He was also suffering from a heart attack. It seems that a combination of circumstances had broken him both financially and physically. Due to bad investments, he'd lost almost all his life savings. On top of this, he had an intense fear of death.

In counseling him, I appealed to his love for his only child, a 15-year-old daughter. I told him that she was entitled to his attention, affection, and devotion. She needed his protection and help to get an education and find her true place in the world. I emphasized that since her mom had passed away when she was born, she needed him to play the role of both father and mother.

I gave him a simple technique: He was to picture himself at home, walking about the house, sitting at his desk, opening mail, answering the phone, and feeling the naturalness and solidity of his daughter's embrace. I suggested that throughout the day he repeat the prayer: "Father, I thank thee for the miraculous healing taking place now. God loves me and cares for me."

He faithfully carried out these instructions. A few weeks later, when he was still in the hospital and picturing himself at his desk at home, something suddenly happened. He said, "I felt lifted up out of the darkness into a blinding light. I felt Divine love filling my soul and was transported from a place of misery to peace of mind." He had a remarkable healing and today is happily leading a successful business life. He has recouped his losses, and his daughter is in college.

When a person is sick or depressed, it's important to guide them to focus on what they care about the most, for love conquers all. *Perfect love casts out fear.* You're what you imagine yourself to be. Therefore, picture yourself as a tremendous success, doing what you long to do. Repeat this visualization over and over again.

⁑✤⁑

A doctor advised a man to give up smoking because it was hurting his blood pressure and heart. The patient began to think about all of the benefits of being a nonsmoker, including better health and greater peace of mind. Then he imagined his doctor congratulating him on his perfect health. He said to himself, "I'm going to give up smoking. I decree it. I'm stopping now. I'm free of this habit and enjoy happiness and peace of mind. I have impeccable health now."

It's said that if you declare something, it shall come to pass and the light shall shine upon your ways. When you make a sincere affirmation, the subconscious accepts it. The smoker therefore ran that mental motion picture through his mind several times a day. He imagined the scene with his physician over and over again, planting the idea of perfect health and tranquility into his subconscious.

He did this for a few weeks and lost all desire to smoke. He went to the doctor, who told him exactly what he'd been affirming. As within, so without; as above, so below; as in heaven (meaning your own mind), so on earth (your body, circumstances, and conditions).

Begin to think constructively and harmoniously and let your words be like a honeycomb—sweet to the ear and good for the spirit. As the Bible says: "A word fitly spoken is like apples of gold in settings of silver." It's beautiful, isn't it? Are your speech, thoughts, and images sweet to the ear? Are you envisioning success and happiness now? If you're going on a trip to Europe, are you imagining a lovely voyage? Are you realizing that the plane is God's idea of moving from point to point freely, joyously, and lovingly? Are you saying, "The pilot is God's creation. She's illumined, inspired, and divinely guided. Love goes before me, making my path straight and perfect. Divine Spirit surrounds and protects the plane. The Holy Presence saturates the hearts and minds of all of the passengers. God controls the highways of the heavens above as well as those of the earth below"? If you're decreeing this and vividly picturing it in your mind, then you're falling in love with the journey and will have a wonderful, wonderful time.

What's your inner speech like at this very moment? Are your thoughts and images sweet to the ear? Perhaps you're saying, "I can't; it's impossible. I'm too old now. What chance do I have? Mary can do it, but I can't. I have no money and can't afford this or that. I've tried, but it's no use." If this is the case, you can see that your words aren't like a honeycomb. There's nothing sweet about those statements. They don't lift you up or inspire you. Never forget the importance of inner speech. It's what you say to yourself when you're alone or before you drift off to sleep. Let the words of your mouth and the meditations of your heart strengthen and sustain you.

Decree now (and say it meaningfully and lovingly): "From this moment forward, I will admit to my mind only those ideas and thoughts that heal, bless, inspire, elevate, and dignify my soul."

⸎

If someone who's sick says, "I'm done for; I have an incurable disease and will never get well," he or she will likely not get better. But if you're in the hospital, imagine yourself at home with your family or back at work at your desk, and you'll quickly recover. A football player who's been injured during a game imagines that he's back on the field, punting the ball. If he didn't have that picture in his mind, he'd never bounce back.

Yes, imagination is the workshop of God. It's a beacon in a world of darkness. What you imagine represents your desire, whether it's a new position or good health. Let your silent thoughts coincide with your feelings. Desire and emotion join together in a mental marriage and will become the answered prayer.

What are you listening to? When you go to sleep at night, are you tuned in to news about murder, crime, burglary, and that sort of thing? Why are you polluting your mind before you go to sleep? Why don't you read the Bible or an inspirational book instead? Fill your mind with eternal verities and go to sleep with the praise of God forever on your lips. Isn't that the way you should drift off? We lie down in peace and know that the Infinite Presence will keep us safe.

Listen to the voice of the One Who Forever Is. What language does It speak? It's not the dialect of any nation or culture but the universal language of love, peace, joy, and harmony. It speaks in faith, confidence, and goodwill; and everyone can understand.

What are you giving your attention to? Whatever you focus on will grow, magnify, and multiply in your experience—whether it's good or bad. Therefore, listen to the great eternal truths.

You've doubtless heard that humankind was made in the image and the likeness of God. This means that your mind is God's mind and your Spirit is God's Spirit. You also use the same laws as Infinite Spirit does to bring forth your thoughts as form, experience, and events.

You can imagine that you're a great singer performing before a distinguished audience make this affirmation:

I am singing for Him. I am poised, serene, and relaxed. The inspiration of the Almighty flows through me, and the song of God wells up within me. The music that comes forth from me fills the souls of all the listeners with joy, happiness, and peace. They are lifted up and inspired because the mood of love, faith, and confidence enters their receptive minds.

Then, of course, you will sing majestically. You've fallen in love with music and have created a new image of yourself. Wonders will unfold as you pray that way.

Your entire world is made after your own likeness and according to your own mental images. Your circumstances are a mirror that reflects your inner thoughts, feelings, and beliefs. If you begin to imagine that evil powers are working against you or that you're jinxed, your deeper mind will respond by creating a reality that corresponds to your negative pictures and fears. You might then begin to say that everything is against you, the stars are opposed to you, or that your bad karma is cursing you . . . but that would be a misunderstanding of the law of mind.

Pain isn't a punishment but a consequence of the misuse of the law of the subconscious. Realize the truth that there's only One Spiritual Power, and It functions through the thoughts and images of your mind. The problems, vexations, and strife in your life are caused by the fact that you've actually wandered after the false gods of fear and error. You must return to the center: the God Presence within.

To focus properly, you need to still the wheels of your mind and enter a quiet, relaxed mental state. You can now put all of your attention on the mental image of your ideal or objective. This process is similar to the way a magnifying glass can be used to start a fire. The rays of the sun are directed by the glass upon an object such a leaf or piece of paper and become increasingly intense until a fire is ignited. Focused, steady attention on your mental images creates a similar mental intensity, making a deep, lasting impression on the sensitive plate of your subconscious mind.

The secret of impregnating the deeper mind is continuous or sustained imagination. When fear or worry comes to you during the day, you can always immediately gaze upon that lovely picture in your mind, knowing that you're using a definite psychological law that's working for you now. As you do this, you're truly watering and fertilizing the seed, thereby accelerating its growth.

⊟✛⊟

The first step in conveying your clarified desire, idea, or image to the deeper mind is to relax and become still. This quiet, peaceful state prevents extraneous matter and false ideas from interfering with your mind's absorption of your idea. Prayer becomes effortless, requiring no mental coercion or willpower. Any time you use mental force, you get the opposite of what you're praying for. This is called the *law of reversed effort.*

In the second step, you begin to imagine what you desire. For example, Lynn L. really wanted to work in the medical field. She took courses in medical assistance and administration at a community college and applied for several positions, but was always rejected because of her lack of previous experience in the field. Nonetheless, she was determined to reach her goal.

Several times a day, she visualized herself in a doctor's office helping with all of the insurance, administrative, and clerical details that take so much time and energy away from dealing directly with patients. Before her next interview, she repeated to herself: "I will get this job. I may not have prior experience, but I know that I'm capable, knowledgeable, and willing to work hard to be an excellent medical assistant."

When Lynn was asked about experience at her next interview, she responded, "I may not have worked in a medical office before, but I've been successful in all of my jobs and have always been able to learn. I know what's expected of an assistant. I've studied and worked hard to prepare for a career in this field, and I'm committed to being the best employee you can find."

The doctor hired her. A few months later, he told her that when he read her application, he'd planned to just give her a courtesy interview and send her on her way, but she impressed him with her enthusiasm and self-confidence. And he added, "I'm glad I found you! You're the best medical assistant I've ever had."

You must know and believe that you're operating a law of mind. You must become convinced that there's a power within you that's capable of manifesting your dreams and visualizations. Become convinced of your God-given ability to use your mind constructively to bring forth the things that you desire. It's all right to build castles in the air, but build a foundation under them. Then you'll bring them to pass.

If you have a clear-cut idea of what you want, the subconscious mind will manifest it. Vividly imagine the fulfillment of your desire in order to give the subconscious something definite to act upon. *Whatsoever ye shall ask in prayer, believing, ye shall receive.*

As you sustain your belief, wonders will begin to unfold and you'll experience the joy of the answered prayer.

In a Nutshell

Your subconscious magnifies and multiplies whatever you give your attention to. As you continue to focus on something, you become compelled to do that thing.

Whatever you attach to the words *I am,* you become. When you look in the mirror and say, "I'm healthy, prosperous, and happy," you're engraving a new self-image in your subconscious mind. The words you send to your deeper mind—your assumptions, beliefs, and convictions—dictate and control all your conscious actions.

You *are* what you imagine yourself to be. Therefore, see yourself as a tremendous success, doing what you long to do. Decree now (say it meaningfully and lovingly): "From this moment forward, I admit to my mind for mental consumption only those ideas and thoughts that heal, bless, inspire, strengthen, elevate, and dignify my soul."

Never forget the importance of inner speech. It's what you silently say to yourself when you're alone or before you fall asleep. Your quiet thought is always made manifest.

The conscious mind is the motor, and the subconscious is the engine. You must start the motor, and then the engine will do the work.

When you have a clear-cut vision of what you wish for, your subconscious mind will bring it to pass. Vividly imagine the fulfillment of your desire and give your deeper mind something definite to act upon.

⊰✦⊱   ⊰✦⊱

Chapter Four

Developing a
Wonderful Personality

*Y*ou can develop a wonderful personality by thinking about whatever is true, honest, just, pure, lovely, and good. If something is praiseworthy, focus on it. You become what you think about all day long; and your personality is the sum total of your thoughts, feelings, beliefs, opinions, early indoctrination, and environmental conditioning.

Your personality is acquired, and you can transform it by focusing on the attributes and power of Divine love, for you're the garment God wears as He moves through the illusion of time and space. Begin now by spending 10 to 15 minutes every morning contemplating this great truth:

> *I am a channel for the light, love, glory, beauty, peace, harmony, and power of the Infinite One. The qualities of God are flowing through me now like a golden river, and I am walking and talking with Infinite Spirit all day long. I am expressing more and more godlike qualities every day of my life. I become what I contemplate, and I am a channel of the Divine now and forevermore.*

As you practice this, wonders will unfold in your life. The first thing you'll learn is that there's no one to change but yourself. This realization is the beginning of a metamorphosis of your entire personality. In addition, start to treat other people as you'd like to be treated. This is the key to happy human relationships in all walks of life. As it says in the Bible: "In everything, do to others what you would want them to do to you. This is what is written in the Law and in the Prophets."

⛬

Are you aware of your inner speech? For example, you may be polite and courteous to people in your office but feel critical and resentful toward them in your mind. Such dark thoughts are highly destructive to you. They're like taking a mental poison that robs you of vitality, enthusiasm, strength, guidance, and goodwill. Remember that whatever you give to someone else, you're also giving to yourself.

Ask yourself now, "What are my thoughts about this other person?" Your inner attitude is what counts. Begin to observe yourself and your feelings about people, conditions, and circumstances. How do you respond to the events and news of the day? You don't have to react negatively to the comments of broadcasters. You can instead remain unruffled, calm, and poised, realizing that they have a right to their expressions and beliefs. It's never what someone says or does that bothers us; it's our *reaction* to what we hear or see that disturbs us.

If someone gossips about you or criticizes you, what's your reaction? Are you going to respond in the typical way by getting flustered, resentful, or angry? If so, you're letting limited thoughts of antagonism, worry, and jealousy get the best of you. You must positively refuse to act in this mechanical, stereotypical way and instead allow the Infinite to express Itself through you. Repeating the following affirmation can help you respond from a place of love:

The Infinite One thinks, speaks, and acts through me now. This is my real self. I am now developing a wonderful personality because in this very moment, I am radiating love, peace, and goodwill to this person who criticized me. I salute the divinity in him or her. God speaks through me as peace, harmony, and love. This attitude is wonderful; and it heals, blesses, and restores my soul.

Instead of responding like the mass of humankind, which returns hate for hate and spite for spite, you can send out love, peace, and goodwill. You can develop a new set of responses to supplant the old ones. If you find yourself always reacting to people, circumstances, and events in the same way, then you're not growing spiritually.

Remember what we said about developing a wonderful personality? It means that you express more and more of the godlike qualities and potencies within you and radiate God's love, harmony, joy, and beauty in your thoughts, words, and actions.

⊭✛⊭

You can become what you want to be by refusing to be a slave to old patterns of thinking. Become a real scientific thinker and practice observing your reactions to the events of the day. Whenever you realize that you're about to respond negatively, say to yourself: "This isn't the Infinite One within me speaking or acting." This will cause you to drop your corrosive thought; and Divine light, love, truth, and beauty will flow through you at that moment.

Instead of getting mired in anger, bitterness, and hatefulness, identify yourself with peace, harmony, and joy. In this way, you practice the Presence of God. Separate yourself from the old attitudes of mind and focus on that which you desire to be. You'll develop a marvelous personality and exude more and more vibrancy. In order to become happy and illumined, you must see yourself as *being* all the qualities you wish to manifest.

Remember this great truth: *You don't have to go along with or believe in negative thoughts or reactions.* Instead, you can respond and think in a new way. If you want to be radiant, healthy, prosperous, and inspired, from this moment forward you must refuse to identify with the pessimistic thoughts that tend to drag you down.

Although most people have heard before that they should see God in others, they may not know that this means becoming aware of the Presence of the Divine in everyone and realizing that Infinite Spirit is expressed through the thoughts, words, and actions of each individual. To really know, accept, and believe these truths is to see God in others.

God is the Father of all and the Life Principle in everybody everywhere. Simply put, He's the highest and best in you. When you show wisdom, truth, and beauty, you're expressing God.

⌗✛⌗

There's no problem in human relations that you can't solve harmoniously and for the benefit of all concerned by using the law of mind. When you say that your associates in the office are cantankerous, mean, or difficult, do you realize that in all probability these attitudes reflect your own inner mental state? Remember that like attracts like and birds of a feather flock together. Isn't it possible that the petulant, critical attitude of your co-workers mirrors your own frustrations and suppressed rage? What they say or do can't really hurt you unless you allow their comments to ruffle you. The only way that you can be annoyed is through your own thoughts about their behavior.

The reason for this is that you're the only thinker in your universe. You alone are responsible for the way you perceive other people. They're not in charge—you are. For example, if someone insults you, you may begin to dwell on what he or she said and decide to get angry and generate a mood of rage. Then you choose to act, perhaps talking back or saying something unpleasant. It takes two to have an argument. You can see that your thoughts, emotions, and reactions all take place in your own mind.

You're the cause of your own anger. If somebody calls you a fool, why should you get mad? You know that you're not an idiot. The person insulting you is undoubtedly mentally disturbed or has serious problems at home. He or she is just as sick as an individual suffering from tuberculosis or cancer. Would you criticize someone with a major illness? Of course you wouldn't—you would offer compassion. Realize that God's peace and Divine love flow through that person's mind. In this way, you can practice the golden rule. You don't identify with rage or hatred but with the law of goodness, truth, and beauty. That's acting with compassion, which is the wisdom of God functioning through the human mind.

People who are hateful, spiteful, or jealous and who say nasty, scandalous things are psychologically ill. How are you going to react to such people? Where's your truth, wisdom, and understanding? Are you going to be just one of the herd and return spite for spite, hate for hate, and anger for anger? No, you can instead stop and affirm: "God sees only perfection, beauty, and harmony in all people everywhere. I see as God sees."

Begin to see all men and women with the compassion of Infinite Spirit. When you identify with Its love and beauty, you won't behold a distorted picture. Would you condemn or criticize someone with a humpback? No, you wouldn't. Perhaps he's suffering from a congenital defect or debilitating illness. Well, there are many people who are *mental* hunchbacks with twisted and distorted minds that were negatively conditioned when they were young. Offer them understanding—for to understand all is to forgive all.

⇥✢⇤

You receive information through your five senses all day long, and *you* determine how you're going to respond to it. You can remain poised and serene or fly into a rage, develop a migraine, or exercise poor judgment. The reason two people react differently to the same situation is due to their subconscious conditioning, which dictates and controls all of their conscious actions. You can recondition your thoughts by identifying yourself with the eternal verities. You can develop a wonderful personality by filling your mind with the concepts of peace, joy, love, happiness, and good-will. If you busy your mind with these ideas, they will sink into the subconscious and become orchids in the garden of God. You're living in Eden, which is simply your deeper mind where you plant seeds or thoughts. You *are* what you think and pray about all day long. What are you focusing on?

No matter how acute a problem may be or how badly a person might behave, in the final analysis there's no one to change but yourself. When you do so, your world will be transformed. Begin with number one: yourself. Remember that you're not living with people but with your *concept* about them. You're living with your beliefs about your husband, wife, children, or acquaintances. What do *you* believe about the individuals in your life? Remember this great truth: God is in all people. Begin to see Divine love in your spouse and friends and call forth the God Presence in all of those around you.

Your subconscious assumptions and convictions about yourself and others dictate and control all of your conscious actions. Don't believe anything that detracts from your health, happiness, and peace of mind because your subconscious *will* faithfully manifest the habitual thoughts of your conscious mind. Whatever you impress on your subconscious mind is inevitably expressed on the screen of space as conditions, experiences, and events. Therefore, cultivate thoughts of peace, happiness, guidance, and goodwill. Meditate on these qualities and accept them with your conscious, reasoning mind. Ask yourself: "What kind of thoughts am I choosing now?"

⊱✦⊰

One time the great Italian tenor Enrico Caruso was struck with stage fright. His throat muscles were constricted with fear, and perspiration poured down his face. He was ashamed because he had to go out onstage in a few minutes but was shaking with terror.

Caruso said, "They will laugh at me; I can't sing." However, then he shouted, "Get out of here limited, fearful self! The Big Me wants to sing through me." By the "Big Me," he meant the unbounded God within or the powers of the subconscious. He continued, "Get out! Get out! The Big Me is going to sing." This released the Almighty Power within him, and when his cue came, he walked out on the stage and sang gloriously, enthralling the audience.

As William James, the father of American psychology, wrote, the subconscious is the power that moves the world—the Almighty Power of God. Your subconscious is one with Infinite Intelligence and boundless wisdom. It's called *the law of life.*

⌘

Laws can be used for either good or bad purposes. For example, you can use the law of electricity to kill someone or light a house—and to fry an egg or vacuum the floor. Surely you wouldn't say that electricity is evil—it all depends on how you use it. Similarly, you can use the law of water to drown a child or quench your thirst, and the law of fire to warm a building or burn someone.

The law of life or your subconscious is also beneficial or harmful depending on how you use it. It's impersonal and nonselective. The deeper mind is like soil. If you put thistle seeds in it, it will grow thistles. If you plant raspberry seeds, you'll get raspberries. You can also plant a negative thought in the soil of your subconscious, and you'll get unpleasant results because the subconscious will express whatever is impressed upon it and bring it to pass.

The reason there's so much chaos, misery, lack, and misfortune in the world is because people don't understand this principle. What are *you* planting in your mind now? What are you choosing in this moment? If you're resentful or hateful, you're sowing seeds of destruction and may develop malignant growths in your body to conform to your negative mental attitude.

The Bible says that "the husband shall be the head of the wife," but it would be foolish to take that statement literally because this timeless book is a psychological, spiritual text dealing with the laws of life. It discusses the male and female principles in each of us. To interpret the biblical terms, the *wife* is the subconscious, which is controlled by the suggestions of the conscious mind, or *husband*. Whatever your conscious mind decrees and believes in, your subconscious will honor and execute accordingly—whether it's good, bad, or indifferent.

⊹✠⊹

The great secret of the ancient mystery schools was that the *I am* in everyone is God. When you say *I am,* you're announcing the presence of the invisible Infinite Mind within you. The *I am* in the Bible means being, life, and awareness. You know that the Almighty Power animates you. No theologian has ever seen spirit, but you've felt the spirit of peace, love, and goodwill well up in you at the sight of your own child.

When you say *I am,* you're announcing the Presence of God in you. Whatever words you add to *I am,* you become. This is the great secret. If you say, "I am a bum and am worthless and inferior," you'll become these things. *I am* is sometimes called the "lost word" because it's used by many people who don't know what they're saying. They state, "I'm blind"; " I'm deaf"; "I'm dumb"; "I'm broke"; "I'm all mixed up"; or "I'm confused." Now wouldn't it be wonderful to say instead: "I am a part of the Living God. I am happy, joyous, and free. I am secure, strong, powerful, loving, harmonious, and kind. I am inspired and illumined. I am absolutely outstanding and a tremendous success"? You will take on all of these qualities because whatever you attach to *I am,* you become.

Whatever is impressed on your subconscious will be expressed on the screen of space as conditions, experiences, and events.

Moses, Isaiah, Jesus, Buddha, Zoroaster, Lao-tzu, and all the illumined seers of the ages proclaimed this truth. Spiritual-minded people who are alert and alive know that the greatest secret in the world is the discovery of the Presence of God within. This is far more important than breakthroughs in the development of nuclear energy, space exploration, or anything else.

⇥✦⇤

Your thoughts and feelings control your destiny regardless of whether you believe it or not. We're dealing with laws of mind that are as incontrovertible as the principles of chemistry, physics, and mathematics. What's the use of arguing that 20 plus 20 equals 50? It doesn't! The intake and the outgo must be equal and motion and emotion must balance. As it is in heaven (which means your own consciousness) so it is on earth (which means your body and environment). This is the law of life.

Realize that the Divine is within you. You're here to let the life and love of God flow through you rhythmically and harmoniously. Pray frequently as follows, and you'll discover wonders unfolding in your life:

> *God flows through me as harmony, health, peace, beauty, and right action. God speaks, thinks, and acts through me now. I am illumined, I am inspired, I am prospered beyond my fondest dreams. I am expressing the life Divine.*

Repeat this simple, beautiful prayer frequently, slowly, quietly, and lovingly. As you do, these seeds (or thoughts) will sink into your deeper mind, which expresses whatever is impressed upon it.

Everyone is capable of something far more wonderful than he or she is presently doing. When you're young, you dream of becoming a hero. To make that dream a reality, you must be taught to express and direct your talents and desires in the right way, along godlike channels.

Something within you tells you that you're born to be victorious and triumphant. God whispers to you through urges and intimations: Go forth and conquer. Infinite Spirit knows that you can do it; otherwise, you wouldn't have the yearning. Your wish to be greater and grander than you are is the push of life within you. Your desire for health is the Life Principle in you telling you that you can be healed. Your longing for wealth is the Higher Self in you guiding you to appropriate God's abundance, which is all around you.

If you want to be prosperous and have all the money you need to do what you want to do when you want to do it, every night before going to sleep say: "God's wealth is circulating in my life, and there is always a Divine surplus." I have taught this all over the world to thousands of men and women, and it works. Repeat that simple phrase three or four times before you drift off to sleep. Your head can be on the pillow and your eyes closed. You're writing this statement with your mental pen—your conscious mind. As you reiterate these truths, they sink down into your subconscious, and your deeper mind will compel you to be wealthy. I say *compel* because the law of your subconscious is compulsion. You'll be inexorably led to be a success and have all the money you desire.

If you're saying, "I can't make ends meet; bills are piling up," and so on, you're planting negative seeds in your subconscious, and the result will be more lack because the subconscious magnifies everything that's deposited into it. If you plant seeds of love, peace, harmony, good humor, abundance, and security, you'll receive a healthy crop of these things.

᪻✛᪻

If the radio in your car stopped working, you wouldn't say that the principles by which radios operate are invalid or that the laws of sound are faulty. Of course not! You'd look for a short circuit and would make the necessary adjustments. In the same way, when you don't get results using your mind, it means that you're not using it the right way or have developed a short circuit. For example, if you criticize the wealth of another person—no matter how it was attained—you'll attract lack and loss in your life because whatever you condemn takes wings and flies away. This is why many people never prosper: They're jealous of the wealth of others. Remember that you're praying for abundance and material riches. How can you prosper when you're finding fault with that which you're praying for? It's simple. Other short circuits include fear, superstition, ill will, and bitterness. To bring love, peace, and happiness into your life, radiate these qualities to everyone. Wish for them health, joy, prosperity, and all the blessings of heaven.

How can you get your subconscious to work for you? First, understand the great secret that the intake and the outgo must be equal. The impression and the expression must be the same. For instance, when you say, "I can't do this"; "I'm too old now"; "I can't meet this mortgage"; "I was born on the wrong side of the tracks"; or "I don't know the right people," you're generating resistance and frustration and are blocking your own good. Affirm boldly: "The God Presence that gave me this desire leads, guides, and reveals the perfect plan to me." This causes the intake and the outgo to be equal. What you feel within is expressed in the without, and you experience prosperity, equilibrium, and joy.

In a Nutshell

You become what you think about all day long. Your personality is the sum total of your thoughts, feelings, beliefs, opinions, early indoctrination, and environmental conditioning. Instead of getting mired in anger, resentment, bitterness, and hatefulness, choose to identify yourself with peace, harmony, and balance. With this attitude, you're practicing the Presence of God. You're separating yourself from the old attitudes of mind and identifying yourself with the new—that which you desire to be. You're developing a wonderful personality and will find that you're exuding more and more vibrancy.

If you want to be peaceful, happy, radiant, healthy, prosperous, and inspired, from this moment forward you must refuse to identify with the negative thoughts that tend to drag you down.

Your mind is a garden of God in which you plant seeds. Regardless of what you sow with your conscious mind, your subconscious will bring it to pass. Therefore, it's wise to cultivate thoughts of harmony, joy, guidance, and goodwill. Meditate on these qualities and accept them in your conscious, reasoning mind . . . and your subconscious will manifest them without question. This is the law of life.

How will you get your subconscious to work for you? Understand the great secret that the intake and the outgo must be equal and that what you impress in your deeper mind manifests in the world. Radiate love, peace, and goodwill to everyone. Wish for them health, happiness, and all the blessings of heaven.

⊱✛⊰ ⊱✛⊰

Chapter Five

Become a Lifter-Upper

*I*n prayer you turn to the Infinite Presence and Power within and contemplate the reality of your vision or dream. When your mind accepts your positive thoughts, you're lifted up and receive courage, strength, and wisdom that transcend the ordinary physical senses. The old state dies and the new is created. Anchor your mind in Divine Power and call upon It. It's responsive and will answer you.

As you focus on the Supreme Intelligence within you, you'll realize that there's a Power that will guide, direct, and respond to you and set you on the high road to happiness, freedom, and peace of mind. You can't manifest your good in a depressed, dejected state but from a place of optimism and faith.

As a rule, you don't rise from the slums and obscurity to attain wealth, honor, and fame through a fluke such as saving someone from drowning or meeting a millionaire who likes you. Remember a simple truth: Your life is always shaped by your character and state of mind. Character is destiny—it's the way you think, feel, and believe and the spiritual values you've enthroned in your mind, including integrity and discipline. These qualities pay dividends.

Release your talents and abilities and develop a zeal for learning more about your inner powers. Then you can lift yourself to astonishing heights.

Energetic, enterprising people who attend to business, do the right thing, and practice the golden rule will make a success of their lives, whether or not they meet a generous stranger, know the right politicians, or win the lottery. Your character and mental attitude will make or break you. Thoughts and feelings create your destiny. It's as simple as that. Your subconscious will bring to pass any idea that is "emotionalized" and felt as true, regardless of whether it's good, bad, or indifferent. Therefore, it's wise to cultivate thoughts that heal, bless, elevate, and dignify your soul.

If you desire to lift yourself up, ask the Divine Power within you to give you what you need—and It will respond to you. Realize that Infinite Intelligence is revealing hidden talents to you, opening up new doors for you, and showing you the way you should go. The Guiding Principle within you will guide you in all your ways.

⊰✦⊱

There are two kinds of people on earth today. These aren't the good and the bad, for it's well understood that the good are half bad and the bad are half good. Nor are they the happy or sad, the rich or poor, or the humble or proud. No, the two types of people I'm referring to are those who lift and those who lean. Wherever you go, you'll find that the world's masses are always divided into just these two classes. And strangely enough, you'll also discover that there's only about 1 lifter-upper for every 20 "leaners." Do you know anyone who depends heavily on others? Which category do you belong to?

You're here to grow, transcend, and discover the Divinity within you. Your purpose is to overcome problems and difficulties—not run away from them—and develop strength, wisdom, and understanding. Without difficulties, you'd never sharpen your mental and spiritual tools. The joy is in triumphing. If a crossword puzzle were filled out for you, it wouldn't be fun. The happiness comes from taking on a challenge. For the same reason, an engineer rejoices in overcoming all the obstacles and failures involved in building a bridge.

Don't let your young children lean on you indefinitely for everything. When they're old enough, teach them to mow the lawn, sell newspapers, and get other odd jobs. Teach them the dignity of labor and the value of getting paid for work well done. This will give them pride in their accomplishment and service to others. It will also teach them self-reliance and confidence in themselves as well as how to see the good in others and call it forth. Then they'll always be lifter-uppers instead of leaners or complainers. In addition, they'll respect and save the money they earn.

You must be careful about how you give to others. Never rob a person of an opportunity to grow and advance. Young people who receive money and help too easily and frequently may fail to develop self-confidence and ingenuity. Constant assistance is destructive to their maturity. Therefore, stop destroying their initiative and demeaning them. Give them an opportunity to discover their inner powers and overcome problems; otherwise, you'll make them dependent and weak, and they'll always seek more handouts.

✢✦✢

A woman I knew paid the rent for a relative, bought groceries for him, and gave him money when he relocated to her town. She wanted to help him until he got a job, but he never did. Rather, he became the perfect leaner. He even resented her because she didn't give him more. When she invited him to a Christmas dinner, he actually stole most of her silver. She cried, "Why did he treat me this way after all I've done for him?" In fact, she didn't do anything to help him.

She'd been seeing him through the eyes of lack and limitation. Her attitude had been: "Poor Tom, he's a stranger here. It's hard for him to get a job." Instead of lifting him up and realizing that he was one with Infinite Intelligence and mentally clothing him with the riches of heaven, what had she done? Figuratively speaking, she'd put him in rags by seeing him as helpless and limited. At the same time, she increased lack and scarcity in her own life, because what you think and feel about another, you create in your own mind and body.

Tom subconsciously picked up the negative attitude of this woman and reacted accordingly. He couldn't respond in any other way. Of course, I advised her to stop filling his refrigerator and let him discover the God Presence within.

You should always be ready to assist those who are really hungry or in need and distress. This is right, good, and true. However, make sure that you don't turn them into parasites. Your support must always be based on Divine guidance, and your motivation should always be to help people help themselves. If you teach them where to find the riches of life, how to become self-reliant, and how to contribute to humanity, they'll never want a bowl of soup, an old suit, or a handout. You need to teach them where the Source is and how to tap into their own subconscious minds. They may have an idea worth a fortune, for within everyone is a vast mine of undiscovered gifts, powers, and riches.

Most of us are willing to lend a helping hand, but it's wrong to contribute to the shortcomings, derelictions, laziness, and apathy of others. There are many able-bodied vagrants who make a living begging for alms. As long as you give to them, they'll never work. They become parasites and leaners. I knew a panhandler in New York who had three homes—in London, Paris, and upstate. He used to laugh at people who would give him a dollar.

❧✦❧

Some young people constantly complain about society and business. They don't like the words *ambition, competition,* and *success,* and they criticize materialism—but there isn't any such thing. Matter is the lowest degree of Spirit, and Spirit is the highest degree of matter. They use credit cards to get a fancy car and buy cell phones, video games, iPods, and everything else. Apparently they like the good things in life, yet at the same time denounce them. That's hypocrisy of the first order. It's like a preacher condemning wealth, then asking for a second collection. You can see how phony that is. Heavens! Some of their parents came over here with no money and couldn't even speak English, but they became great engineers, doctors, and scientists. They contributed so much to this country.

Our history is replete with examples of such men and women who rose from poverty and misery to become leaders of industry or government. They didn't give up when faced with obstacles, but worked hard to overcome them. Dave Thomas, the man who founded the Wendy's Old Fashioned Hamburgers fast-food chain is an example of such a man. As an orphan, he was adopted by a poor family. His adoptive mother died early in his childhood, and his adoptive father, an itinerant laborer, never stayed in one place long enough to establish roots. Thomas had to go to work at a young age, most frequently doing menial labor in restaurant kitchens.

He became intrigued with the restaurant industry and dreamed of someday owning his own dining establishment. Despite the hardship of his poverty and unstable family life, he never gave up his desire. He planted his goal in his subconscious mind and continued to work toward it in the face of many setbacks.

By working in almost all capacities in restaurants, Thomas learned about every aspect of the business. He became an expert cook, a competent marketer, and a top customer-service provider. In due course, he became the manager of a Kentucky Fried Chicken outlet. His great success in this position enabled him to obtain backing to open his own business, which ultimately became one of the most profitable fast-food chains.

Despite his accomplishments, he never forgot his beginnings. Because of his need to work to support himself, he'd had to drop out of high school. But after he achieved business success, he encouraged young people in challenging circumstances to continue their schooling. He set an example by earning his own high school diploma more than four decades after he'd left school. He wanted to demonstrate that it's never too late to graduate.

"I tell people to program their minds to get all the education they possibly can. The fact that I got my diploma 45 years after dropping out shows that it's never too late," said Thomas. "Even with everything that's happened in my life, getting this diploma is one of my most important accomplishments."

In addition to his work in the field of education, he became a leading advocate for adoption. He donated millions of dollars and spent much of his time working with adoption services and lobbying to obtain more equitable laws in this area. In 1992 he founded the Dave Thomas Foundation for Adoption. He wasn't motivated by selfish desires or a yearning for power, but by a wish to help others learn to program their minds for success and overcome problems as he had done.

You can also achieve what Dave Thomas did—in your own way. You're here to contribute, whether by pulling an oar or driving a car. Life rewards faith, courage, endurance, stick-to-itiveness, and persistence. It's through overcoming obstacles that you develop character . . . and character is destiny. Lean on the Divine Presence within you rather than on other people or the government, which can't give you anything unless it first takes it away from you. Furthermore, no politician can legislate peace, joy, abundance, security, wisdom, neighborly love, equality, or goodwill. How frightfully dumb can people be to believe that someone can give them these qualities!

You create all good things and can give yourself security. The government is your own mind: an administration of Divine ideas mothered by Infinite love. It's the leadership of the free. No one else in the entire world can guarantee you freedom, peace of mind, or health. These come from the spiritual world within you.

꽤✛꽤

Leaners coast along on their name, background, heredity, or good looks until people become aware of how empty they are inside. Then they collapse because they have no inner strength. What truly supports you is your faith, confidence, and trust in the powers of your subconscious mind. For instance, a business executive in Los Angeles told me that in October 1929, he and his brother lost everything in the stock-market crash. Each of them had been worth over $1 million. His brother committed suicide by jumping out of a window because he believed that he'd lost everything and that there was nothing to live for.

The business executive told me that he said to himself, "I've lost money. So what? I have good health, a lovely wife, abilities, and talents. I have the wisdom that I've garnered through the years and financial acumen. I'll make money again." He rolled up his sleeves and went to work. He watered gardens, mowed lawns, washed automobiles, and did a lot of odd jobs. He accumulated money, reinvested it, and became immensely wealthy again in a short period of time. A person's skills, wisdom, and experience can't be taken away. That's where the true riches are.

He was a lifter-upper and knew that Divine Power would reveal a solution. He called upon the spiritual reserves within him and received strength, courage, wisdom, and guidance. This man also gave financial advice to others, and they made a small fortune, too. When you make money for others, you make it for yourself.

Infinite Intelligence is responsive and will answer when you call. You and this Almighty Source are one. Don't rely on land, stocks, the government, your background, heredity, or anything else. Trust the Supreme Wisdom within you to sustain you and watch over you at all times. The pearl of great price is in your own mind.

᠁✛᠁

Stop looking outside yourself for answers, for that's denying the riches of the Divine within you. You're stealing power, wisdom, and intelligence *from yourself.* The Living Spirit that created you is the Source of all things—even the air you breathe—and has all of the solutions you need.

The whole world was here when you were born. Yes, all of the cattle on a thousand hills; the sun, moon, and stars; the oceans;

and the gold in the land were already here when you were born. Life was a complete gift to you, and you're here to release the imprisoned splendor and talents that are within you. If you think that you're here to earn a living, that's all you'll ever do. But your existence is an unlimited blessing. It was never born and will never die. Believe in yourself as a spiritual being of grandeur and recognize your Divinity. Moreover, contemplate the truth that you're here to release the glory that's within you.

Be a lifter-upper by realizing that Infinite Power supports you. This Source will lift you up; open new doors for you; give you new, creative ideas; heal and inspire you; and provide a sense of deep, abiding security in that which never changes and is the same yesterday, today, and forever. All you have to do is trust this Presence and believe in It, and wonders will unfold in your life.

The lifter-uppers meet challenges head-on. They say to themselves, "This problem is Divinely outmatched. There's a difficulty here, but the Supreme Intelligence is present, too, and It always wins." They meet all hurdles and obstacles with faith, courage, and confidence. They go forth to conquer sickness, fear, and ignorance.

⛭✝⛭

According to an old saying, a weak chick gets pecked to death by the healthy ones. This is true. The boy in school who feels beaten, defeated, and rejected gets picked on by the bullies. Why? Because he feels inferior and inadequate and is full of fear. He's saying to himself, "I'm no good." But when he stands up to his tormentors, challenges them, and meets them head-on, they always retreat.

Everybody is a child of the Living God. Feel your dignity and grandeur as a blessed being and realize that you're immune to the insults, criticism, and vilification of others because you're Divinely born. If you exalt and love the Holy Presence within you, everyone—even your so-called enemies—will be constrained to do you good.

Refuse to accept suffering and never resign yourself to any situation. You're a transcendental being, and can mentally lift yourself above all conditions and circumstances. When Abraham Lincoln was informed that his secretary of war was maligning him and calling him an ignorant baboon, he replied, "That man is the greatest secretary of war this country has ever had." No one could hurt Lincoln or wound his ego because he knew where his strength was and that no one could drag him down unless he allowed it through the actions of his own mind. Lincoln recognized the Divine Presence within and lifted himself up, thereby acquiring the strength to uplift the whole country.

If someone criticizes or condemns you and calls you a skunk, how do you react? How could an insult upset you unless you allow it? Nobody can hurt you but yourself. Where there's no opinion, there's no suffering. If a cucumber is bitter, don't eat it.

❈✛❈

Do you get riled up about the headlines in the morning news? Are you in a state of turmoil? If you keep it up, all it will get you is an ulcer, high blood pressure, or indigestion. Who makes you sick? Not the columnists or reporters. You do it to yourself. They're entitled to write what they want and have the right to think as they do—and you have the freedom to write letters to the editor and refute anything you read.

Do your in-laws disturb you? Are you saying, "He doesn't believe what I think he should" or "She doesn't act the way I think she should"? Well, why should they conform to your beliefs? They're adults! And if what they think or do begins to worry you, you're going to get sick and end up on a psychiatrist's couch.

❈✛❈

Maybe you've heard about preachers who denounce alcohol, believing that it's the only evil in the world. In fact, drinking is just a bad habit. Evil is in the mind, not in the alcohol. The beverage only has the power you give to it. You can break the bottle and pour it down the sink. The power is in you. Nonetheless, these preachers rant and rave that all the whiskey in town should be thrown into the river. You see how silly the whole thing is. There's no one to change but yourself, and your real self is God. Exalt, honor, and respect this Divine Presence within you.

When you love the Living Spirit within you, you'll automatically respect the Divinity in the police officer, the college professor, your mother, your father, and neighbors because you'll realize that everyone is an incarnation of Infinite Spirit. We're all interdependent. You may need a doctor, lawyer, psychologist, or carpenter, and they may need you. Let's remember to lift up God in everyone and see each person as a child of the Divine—radiant, joyous, prosperous, and free.

As you love and exalt the Divinity within yourself, you'll automatically exalt it in others. If you're married and you don't honor this Infinite Presence within yourself, you won't be able to respect or love your spouse.

Don't tell me that you can love the person next door unless you first cherish the Living Presence within you. Your neighbor is the closest thing to you. He or she is also part of the Spirit that started your heartbeat, grows hair on your face, and created the world.

※✝※

Some people today despise success. Don't listen to them! Yes, you should have ambition and want to achieve something. You were born to succeed in your prayer life, relationships, and communion with the Divine. If you're a doctor, you want to become a great one so that you can save thousands of lives. You don't want to be mediocre. Whether you're a chemist, engineer, teacher, or manager, you want to excel so that you're able to help humanity.

Seek and ye shall find. Yes, you'll discover sermons in stones, songs in brooks, and God in everything, for there's only Infinite

Spirit. The lifter-upper knows the truth of this ancient saying: "What thou seest, that, too, become thou must: God if thou seest God, and dust if thou seest dust."

Stop crawling and living in the shadows and eddies of life. Exalt the Divine in the midst of you. God is with you now.

In a Nutshell

Character is destiny. It's the way you think, feel, and believe and the spiritual values you have enthroned in your mind, including integrity and discipline. These qualities pay dividends. Release your talents and abilities and develop a zeal for learning more about your inner powers. You can then lift yourself to astonishing heights.

Thought and feeling create your destiny. Your subconscious will bring to pass any idea that you "emotionalize" and feel as true, whether it's good, bad, or indifferent. Therefore, it's wise to choose thoughts that heal, bless, inspire, elevate, and dignify your soul.

You're here to grow, transcend, and discover the Divinity within you. Your purpose is to overcome difficulties and challenges—not run away from them. The joy comes in triumphing over problems.

Be a lifter-upper by realizing that Infinite Power supports you. This Source will lift you up; open up new doors for you; give you new, creative ideas; and provide you with a sense of deep, abiding security in that which never changes and is the same yesterday, today, and forever. All you have to do is trust this Presence and believe in It, and wonders will unfold in your life.

Some people today despise achievement, but don't listen to them. Yes, you should have ambition and desire success. You were born to succeed in your prayer life, relationships, and communion with the Divine.

❧❧ ❧❧

Chapter Six

---•◆•---

There Are Certain
Things You Can't Change

*P*rayer is the contemplation of the truths of God from the highest standpoint. It transforms situations, circumstances, and the one who prays. We become that which we focus on; and as we meditate on harmony, beauty, love, peace, Divine guidance, and goodwill, the entire world magically melts into the image and likeness of our thoughts.

Some years ago when Nikita Khrushchev was the leader of the Soviet Union and visited America, a woman wrote to me saying that she was going to pray for him to cause him to change and become peaceful and loving toward the United States. She thought that by sending out vibrations of love and harmony to Mr. Khrushchev, he'd experience a mental transformation. However, her approach was all wrong.

I explained to her that the only person she could change was herself and that she could begin by regularly and systematically practicing the presence of God by reiterating the following great truths until they sank into her subconscious mind:

I am Divinely guided in all ways. I think, speak, act, and react from the standpoint of the Indwelling God. I meditate on those things that are true, lovely, noble, and godlike. I contemplate Divine law and order in my life. Heavenly love fills my soul. Spiritual right action reigns supreme. I know that all of my thoughts tend to manifest themselves in varying degrees in my life and that I am compelled to express and radiate that which I think about all day long. Together with others, I generate a mighty spiritual force that neutralizes the mental poisons of the mass mind.

The Bible says: "Let God arise, let His enemies be scattered; let them also that hate Him flee before Him." This means that you need to resurrect the light, truth, and love of God in your own mind and heart in order to destroy the enemies of fear, hate, jealousy, greed, anger, doubt, and self-condemnation. All of these are poisons that you generate in your own mind, but you can eradicate them by sowing thoughts of harmony, love, and peace. Your spiritual vibrations will be poured out on all of humankind, thereby reducing the delusions and pessimism of the mass mind.

Praying for someone is vastly different from trying to change that person. For example, if your mother asked you to pray for her to overcome cancer, you'd accept her request and contemplate the Infinite Healing Presence flowing through her as harmony, beauty, joy, and vitality. By dwelling on the wholeness and perfection of God and His Divine love, you would rise in consciousness until you entered into the mental conviction that a healing would take place; and according to your belief, it would be done unto you. Your mom's subconscious would be open and receptive to the idea of perfect health and receive your prayer, for there's no time or space in the One Mind. If you really *believe* what you claim to be true, it will come to pass.

⇥✦⇤

A few years ago I was told about a woman who was incensed because the occupant of the hotel room next to hers was playing music every morning, afternoon, and night. The hotel manager informed her that it was the great Carteau, a famous French pianist, practicing for his concert. "Oh!" she exclaimed. "I have tickets for that performance. I'm going to invite my friends to my room to listen to him." Nothing had changed but her attitude. The hotel, the music, and the atmosphere were the same. The only thing that was different was her perception of the situation.

⊭✟⊭

You can't change the tides, the rotation of the Earth, the movement of the sun, or the order of the galaxies in space. You can't guide the planets in their orbits, interfere with the four seasons, or alter weather patterns around the world. The reason for this is obvious: God works on the cosmic or universal plane, while we humans work on the individual plane. In other words, God or Universal Intelligence will do nothing for you except through your thoughts, imagery, and convictions. In order for God to work on the individual plane, you have to direct your thoughts along specific lines using affirmative prayer. That's modern science today.

I visited a man in the hospital who'd undergone a major operation and whose kidneys had completely stopped functioning. He asked me to pray for him, saying, "I have no future. I'm only 40, but I suppose I'm done for. What will happen to my family? Prayer is all that's left."

I explained to him that the first step was to sincerely and willingly believe that the Cosmic Healing Power that made his body and all of his organs could restore and heal him. I gave him this prayer:

I live in the awareness that the Infinite Healing Presence, which made my body and knows its every process, is permeating all of the atoms of my being, making me whole and perfect. My kidneys are God's idea, and through the power of the Almighty, they are working perfectly now.

After about 15 minutes, his prayer was answered and his kidneys began to function, which pleased his surgeon immensely. He's now back with his family and in perfect health. While conferring with me recently, he said, "My future is assured. I know that my present thoughts shape what unfolds in my life." Of course, this is absolutely true. This man knows that his faith in the goodness and guidance of God will always manifest blessings in his life. With this attitude, he's building a glorious future for himself that's full of harmony, health, peace, and abundance.

There are certain things that you can't change, but you *can* transform yourself and mold your own future. Your thoughts and feelings create your destiny—whether you know it or not.

⊣✟⊢

A few years ago while lecturing in Belfast, I interviewed a young woman who said to me, "I don't have the power to handle my problems or solve the difficulties of life. I'm divorced, hate myself, and am no good."

I explained to her that her condition was simply due to habitual negative thinking, constant criticism, and self-condemnation, which were poisoning her wells of faith, confidence, and enthusiasm and rendering her a physical and mental wreck. In other words, she was polluting the sanctuary of the Living God within her—her own mind.

I told her a story about Eddie Rickenbacker, a fighter pilot and hero during World War I. He and his companions were shipwrecked and set adrift on a raft in the Pacific Ocean. Rickenbacker prayed for food, and a seagull came and perched on his head. It remained long enough to be seized and utilized for food. He also prayed to be rescued, and—of course—he and his friends were eventually saved. He believed in the wisdom and power of God to take care of him. When you have faith and ask for help, Infinite Power responds. *Call upon me; I will answer you. I will be with you in trouble. I will set you on High, because you have known my name.* The word *name* in the

Bible always means "nature." The nature of Infinite Intelligence is to respond to your call.

This story made a profound impression on the young Irish woman. I explained that she could recondition her mind and that when she had any kind of pessimistic or self-denigrating thought (which she inevitably would because of her destructive habit), she was to immediately supplant it with affirmations about her spiritual self-worth and beauty. I also gave her the following prayer to repeat out loud for about ten minutes in the morning and at night:

> *I am a child and channel of God. Infinite Spirit needs me to be where I am; otherwise, I would not be here. I know I am on Earth to express more of God's love, life, truth, and beauty. I am here to do my share and to contribute to humanity. I have a lot to offer. I can give love, laughter, joy, confidence, and goodwill to all people, animals, and things in God's universe. I am here to stir up the gift of Divine Presence within me. And whatever I give to life, life returns to me magnified, multiplied, and running over.*
>
> *I deposit in the garden of my mind wonderful seeds of peace, wisdom, success, harmony, and happiness. I forgive myself for harboring negative, destructive thoughts; and I pour out love and goodwill to all of my relatives and to people everywhere. I know when I have forgiven others, because when I meet them in my mind, there is no sting. I no longer feel angry and resentful. I am free. I am constantly partaking of the fruit of the delightful seeds I am planting in my subconscious, which is called <u>Eden</u> or the <u>garden of God.</u> I know that my thoughts, like seeds, will manifest as form, experience, and conditions. I think about these things, and the Cosmic Power within me brings it all to pass. I am at peace.*

She repeated the above prayer and experienced wonderful changes in her life. She wrote to me about her transformation in the following letter:

Dear Dr. Murphy:

We all enjoyed your lectures in Belfast. You opened the eyes of many people. I'd like to tell you about the change that's come over me. I prayed the way you told me to, and after a few days, all of the bitterness in my soul disappeared as if by magic. I joined a dancing class and have been promoted to the position of department head in my store. The assistant manager proposed to me, and we're going to be married in six months. I've forgiven myself and my relatives. Every day is a new day. I know that I create my own future by the way I think, feel, and imagine. I'm grateful, and it's fantastic!

—☩—

Universal Wisdom governs the entire world, regulating the atmosphere and meeting the needs of all people throughout the world. You can't change God. How could you? He's the same yesterday, today, and forever. You must find out what's true about Infinite Presence and align yourself with Its universal principles, which existed before any human walked this earth or a single church was built. The truths of God are immutable and eternal. You must become a channel through which the light, love, truth, beauty, and peace of the Almighty endlessly flow.

—☩—

A woman came to me feeling distraught, depressed, and guilty because her son-in-law had shot someone in the neighborhood. I explained to her that she wasn't responsible for the actions or state of mind of another person and that if she began to worry and fulminate about all the sociopaths and sex offenders in the country, she'd make herself sick, because you become what you contemplate. I added that her business in life is to walk in the awareness of God's love and peace, thereby generating a mood of harmony, serenity, and beauty in the world. These spiritual vibrations tend to minimize and neutralize the noxious patterns of fear, hate, jealousy, and greed in the mass or race mind.

I pointed out to her that creating a wailing wall of depression and guilt within herself would most likely contaminate and poison her life and contribute to the misery and suffering of humankind. She thereupon absolved herself from a sense of guilt and walked out a free woman into the sunshine of God's love.

You must be careful to not let demagogues try to make you feel guilty because of crimes or wrongs committed by somebody else. Why should *you* feel guilty? You can't control the words or actions of others and aren't guilty because John Jones shot his wife. You must not permit others to manipulate your mind for ulterior purposes. Your mission in life is to live in the consciousness of Divine love, knowing that with your eyes on God, there's no evil on your path.

I received a beautiful Christmas card from a member of our organization that contained a prayer that you can use to stay focused on the peace of God:

> *God, give us grace to accept with serenity*
> *the things that cannot be changed,*
> *courage to change the things that should be changed,*
> *and the wisdom to distinguish the one from the other.*

Alcoholics Anonymous and other self-help groups use a version of this passage, which is often called *the serenity prayer.*

꿔✞꿔

The Bible says: "Acquaint now thyself with Him and be at peace: thereby good shall come unto thee." Get to know the God Presence within you. It's the Living Spirit in you that can never be sick, frustrated, or vitiated in any way. It was never born and will never die. Let the Infinite ocean of peace, joy, and wisdom flow through you, and you'll discover that you can stay healthy in any kind of weather. If you're fearful and worried and say, "The night air gives me a chill" or "I'll catch my death of cold if my feet get wet," you're simply decreeing sickness and suffering for yourself. The night air never gave anyone pneumonia or a virus. Millions of people don't get the flu, aches, pains, sniffles, or rheumatism when it gets cold. Therefore, it's not universal law. If it were, everyone would be afflicted by changes in the weather. No, these illnesses are obviously due to the mental and emotional climate of people's own minds. You must remember that health and well-being are of God—yesterday, today, and forever.

In Proverbs, it says: "The Fear of the Lord is the beginning of knowledge." *Fear* can be defined as "being afraid," but it also has another meaning: a wholesome reverence for something. Give all of your respect and power to the Infinite Presence within you. The peace of the Everlasting God fills your heart. It's a lamp unto your feet and a light upon your path. God is the love that imbues your soul and the healing presence that animates and sustains you. The Divine light permeates every atom of your being so that your whole body dances with the rhythm of the Eternal God.

In a Nutshell

There are certain things that you can't change, but you *can* transform yourself and shape your own future. Whether you know it or not, your thoughts and feelings create your destiny.

When you're filled with doubt about taking a stand in a given situation, pray: "God grant me the courage to change the things that can be changed, the serenity to accept the things that cannot be changed, and the wisdom to know the difference."

Your mission in life is to walk in the awareness of God's love and peace, thereby generating a mood of peace, love, and harmony for the entire world. These spiritual vibrations tend to minimize and neutralize the noxious patterns of fear, hate, jealousy, and greed in the mass or race mind.

There's no sense in stirring up the mental poisons of grief, sorrow, hostility, and depression within yourself and exuding that harmful mental effluvia into the mass mind, which is already contaminated enough.

Keep your eyes on God, knowing that there's no evil on your path.

⊱✦⊰ ⊱✦⊰

Chapter Seven

Learning to Say Yes and No in Life

Two of the most important words in the world are *yes* and *no*. It's your obligation to say yes to all ideas that heal, bless, and inspire; to accept only eternal truths; and to use spiritual concepts in your life.

You must say no to all teachings, thoughts, creeds, and dogmas that inhibit, restrict, and instill fear into your mind. In other words, accept nothing that doesn't fill your soul with happiness. Realize that God is Infinite Love and Life and that He's expressing the fullness of His joy right now. God is wisdom, and your intellect is constantly anointed with the light from On High. God is peace, and you're expressing more and more Divine harmony in your thoughts, words, and deeds every day.

As you make a daily habit of realizing these truths, you'll develop a radiant personality and create a channel for all good things to flow to you.

❧✠❧

The Bible says: "Every valley shall be exalted, and every mountain and hill shall be made low: and the crooked shall be made straight, and the rough places plain." When you're in the valley of despair, turn to the God Presence within you and realize that external events and circumstances aren't causative. Conditions don't create other conditions. The primary cause—that which forms your destiny—is your thoughts and feelings or mental attitude. Therefore, decree that Infinite Intelligence reveals the solution. Contemplate the way you *want* things to be, and the mountains and hills (problems) shall be lowered (eradicated).

As you claim that Divine law and order govern your life, the crooked (the ups and downs of life) shall be made straight and the rough places plain; that is, you'll begin to experience growth, achievement, and advancement and be free of detours, sickness, accidents, and losses—as well as foolish expenditures of energy, time, and effort. As you keep your eyes on the God Power and tune in to the Infinite Wisdom within you, all barriers, delays, and difficulties will disappear, and the desert of your life will fully rejoice and blossom like a rose.

Say yes to the following beautiful biblical injunction: "Finally, brethren, whatever things are true, whatever things are noble, whatever things are just, whatever things are pure, whatever things are lovely, whatever things are of good report, if there is any virtue and if there is anything praiseworthy—meditate on these things."

You should completely reject anything you hear or read that doesn't conform to these spiritual laws—even a lecture from your minister, priest, imam, or rabbi. Give an emphatic and decisive *no* to any thoughts or suggestions of fear, worry, resentment, ill will, bitterness, or hostility. Remember that what you say yes to in life is deposited in your subconscious mind and eventually comes forth as experiences, conditions, and events. What you say no to ceases to be part of your life.

⊨✦⊨

I recently talked with Mary, a woman employed in a large office. Five o'clock was quitting time, but her co-workers regularly asked her to stay late to complete *their* tasks. One would say, "Mary, I have an appointment with the chiropractor. Will you finish these letters for me?" Another would tell her that she had an appointment with the dentist or doctor and needed to leave early. And someone else would claim that he had to get to the airport to meet relatives . . . and so on. She agreed to take on all of their work even though she deeply resented it.

Mary had to learn to say no. She finally realized that these selfish people were pulling the wool over her eyes, taking advantage of her, pushing her around, and laughing at her behind her back. She therefore decided to make plans for herself after work; and when her colleagues asked her to stay overtime, she told them that it was impossible because she had to keep her own appointments. From that point on, she no longer allowed other people to take advantage of her. It's wrong to let others manipulate you or steal from you. Learn to say no to everything that's false.

᛭

A woman told me that she babysat her grandchild three nights a week, neglecting her own children and husband. Her son and daughter-in-law came home at one or two o'clock in the morning— usually drunk. They gave her no thanks and showed no appreciation, yet she believed that she had an obligation to take care of the toddler. I explained to her that it was morally and spiritually wrong for her to contribute to their selfishness, boorishness, and delinquency, and that she needed to put her husband and family first. I suggested that the next time her son asked her to babysit, she should emphatically say, "No! Get a babysitter and pay her to do it." She did this, and from then on her son and daughter-in-law had far more respect for her and no longer took advantage of her.

᛭

A man who wrote a manuscript and sent it to several publishers in New York had it returned to him marked "No comment." One editor performed what the writer called "mayhem" on his manuscript, which made him furious. He was incensed, but when he learned about the power of thought, he began to use the laws of mind constructively. He reasoned as follows: *This manuscript contains a lot of useful information and is extremely good. Infinite Intelligence reveals to me the ideal publisher who will appreciate the contents and agree to publish it in Divine order.* He learned to say yes to life, and in a few weeks, he received news from a publisher that his manuscript had been accepted.

When someone turns you down or a company rejects your application, you don't have to accept defeat. You can completely dismiss it and realize that the Infinite Intelligence within you opens a door that no one can shut.

⇥✟⇤

A woman told me recently that she and her sister had had an argument on the phone. Her sister had called her a jerk and hung up. The woman became furious, entered into despondency and gloom, and had what she described as a "slow burn." I explained to her the workings of her mind and said, "So your sister said you're a jerk. Ask yourself: <u>*Am*</u> *I one? Do I have any inconsiderate tendencies?* If the answer within you is no, why should you be disturbed?

I told the woman that her sister had no ability to hurt her and that the real power was in the movement of her own thoughts and emotions. All she had to do was bless her sister and go on about her business. She prayed: "I fully and freely forgive my sister and wish for her all of the blessings of life. Any time I think of her, I say to myself, 'God be with you.'" After a few days using this simple prayer, she had a complete healing.

When you get angry and resentful, you become enmeshed in a negative, destructive state. However, it's possible for you to remain completely aloof and detached instead . You can rise above any abuse and reject anything of a hurtful nature. All you have to do is enter into the secret place of the Most High. Tune in to the Infinite and affirm boldly: "I am identified with the peace, harmony, and love of God, which flow through me now." You can refuse to come down from that impregnable position for any person in this world.

Remember that no one can hurt you but yourself. The statements and actions of others have absolutely no power to disturb you. If a cucumber is bitter, you don't have to eat it. If someone calls you a snake in the grass, it's easy for you to say, "God's peace fills your soul," and walk on.

❧✠❧

Peter Ouspensky, a prominent Russian philosopher and writer of the early 20th century, used to ask students who got upset about the insults, gossip, and actions of other people, "Is there truth in what that individual said?" If the answer was no, Ouspensky would say, "Well, then, why should you be disturbed? Stay focused on your purpose." What is *your* purpose? To identify mentally and emotionally with harmony, peace, wisdom, understanding, success, right action, and beauty. It's as simple as that.

There's an old saying: "Those whom the gods wish to destroy, they first make mad." If someone can get you riled up, that person has power over you. Under the sway of negative emotion, you're bound to do something stupid that you don't really want to do but which you rashly rush into because of your volatile feelings. When you're in tune with the Infinite, you're in an impenetrable fortress that no one can attack. You're alone in the silence that is God.

❧✠❧

A young man who was studying New Thought teachings in order to become a minister told me that his mother created a lot of drama at home. She'd have weeping and fainting spells and exclaim, "You're giving me a heart attack because you're leaving the faith of your father, the only true religion! Someday I'll die, and you'll be sorry." She'd have many tantrums throughout the day.

I explained to this man that his mom's motivation was to stop him from fulfilling his heart's desire. She wanted to get her own way and was trying to make him feel guilty because he wouldn't conform to her wishes. This is emotional blackmail. I told him that he should absolutely refuse to yield to her tirades and tears. He only had to say no.

So he went to his mother and said, "Mom, these teachings are giving me a new lease on life and an inner sense of peace and happiness that I've never had before. I've also had a marvelous healing of a physical condition that I endured for many years. If you really love me, you'll rejoice that I've found serenity and joy and wish me well."

Love isn't possessive and isn't about trying to force someone to do what *you* want or to believe what you believe. The son continued, "Mom, I'm going to stand my ground and become a New Thought minister. What gives me peace and harmony must of necessity give peace and harmony to you."

After several months, she wrote him a beautiful letter telling him how grateful and happy she was that he'd found his true place in life and that she wished for him all the blessings in the world.

When you know that something is true, don't try to appease the other person. Always stand on eternal principles and never yield one iota. You can't satisfy someone who's a little Hitler in his or her heart. Appeasement never wins gratitude.

─╬─

One of my students told me recently that he'd been a guest in a home, and his hostess had begun to criticize his beliefs about reincarnation, karma, and life after death. She said that he must be stupid beyond words not to realize that people come back again and again to expiate the sins and crimes they committed in former lives. She was furious that he didn't agree with her.

He politely told her, "You have complete freedom to believe in all these things, and I'm glad if your beliefs give you solace and comfort. However, I hope that you don't want to impose your ideas on me because I find them repugnant and can't accept them. I expect you to give me the same freedom I give you." This is the proper approach to saying yes to the truth and no to that which is false.

‑¤✧¤‑

A few months ago I received a six-page letter from a woman vilifying and denouncing me because I said that there's no hell, limbo, or purgatory, and that the only hell that exists is the one we create in our own mind (which, of course, is absolutely true).

She'd gone through the Bible—both the Old and New Testaments— picking out all of the quotations referring to Satan, the devil, the "adversary," and so on. In scanning the letter, I realized that I was dealing with a sick mind. I simply blessed her, threw the letter into the wastebasket, and went on to the next one. How could a piece of paper with some ink on it have any power over my mood or thoughts?

The only influence people can have over you is the influence you give them in your own mind. You have the freedom to bless or curse them. *To bless* means to say yes to life and to wish for others everything you desire for yourself, including harmony, health, peace, and love.

‑¤✧¤‑

It's necessary to have a sense of humor about the things that happen. If you don't laugh at yourself at least six to eight times every day, you'll never grow spiritually.

‑¤✧¤‑

A priest said to a rabbi, "Sometimes I think that I behold the Christ in you." The rabbi replied, "That in you which enables you to see the Christ in me is that in me which sees the Jew in you." Let's realize that we're all children of the one Father. We have one common progenitor: God or the Life Principle.

The Bible says: "Have we not all one Father? Has not one God created us?" This means that we're all intimately related. Actually, we're all brothers and sisters. Say yes to your unity with God, which is the Living Spirit Almighty within you. It doesn't have a face, form, or figure, but is the Infinite Presence within. Say no to all who would deny this. Also say yes to the following prayer:

> God *is*, and His Presence flows through me as love, peace, harmony, joy, beauty, wisdom, light, understanding, security, and true expression. I am a focal point for the Divine. All of the qualities and attributes of Infinite Spirit are being expressed through me in every moment of my life, and I become more god-like in all of my ways. I am a beloved child of God.

We're all children of the Most High. If you repeatedly affirm this great truth, you'll develop a wonderful personality and miracles will unfold in your life. You'll exude vibrancy and become flooded with the radiance of limitless light. Whenever any fear or worry comes to you or whenever you think you can't accomplish something, get still and quiet and contemplate the sovereignty of Spirit. Realize that Infinite Intelligence is within you and that God is boundless love, infinite life, marvelous wisdom, absolute power, and complete harmony. Nothing can oppose this Divine Presence or challenge It.

If you call upon God, He answers you. He responds to your thoughts—every modern scientist knows this is true. Affirmative prayer will quiet your mind and completely relax you. When you're in this state of repose, contemplate what you want to be, do, or have, and the Infinite Spirit within you will respond to your faith and confidence in It.

Remember a great truth: *Nothing is forever. Everything passes away.* Scientific thinkers don't give power to any created thing because they know that God is greater than their thought, just as the artist is greater than the art. The spiritually minded person also knows that there's only one Creator and that everything is subject to change. You should therefore give all of your allegiance and devotion to the Divine Presence within you. No one's ever seen Spirit, but you can feel Its essence of joy, love, and ecstasy in your own heart. When your thoughts are God's thoughts, His power is with your desire for good. Don't make a god of any person, place, or thing, for there's only one God—not two, three, or four. From the rising of the sun to the setting of the same, there's nothing else.

⊹

Suppose you went to a sailor on a ship and said, "I notice yellow pigmentation around your eyes. You look pale and weak and seem as if you're going to become seriously ill." Since he's full of confidence and faith that he'll have a wonderful time at sea, he'd dismiss your comments. He might even think that you're mentally unbalanced. He knows that he's immune to seasickness and that he can roll with the waves and feel the rhythm of the deep.

You're a master and are in charge of your own conceptive realm: your thoughts, feelings, emotions, and reactions. When any negative suggestion comes to you, say: "God's love fills my soul. I am in the secret place of the Most High. The Lord is my shepherd; I shall not want. Goodness and mercy follow me all the days of my life, for I dwell in the house of God forever."

In a Nutshell

It's your obligation to say yes to all ideas that heal, bless, and inspire; to accept only eternal truths; and to use spiritual concepts in your life.

You must say no to all teachings, ideas, thoughts, creeds, and dogmas that inhibit, restrict, and instill fear into your mind.

Love isn't possessive and doesn't try to force other people to believe what you believe or coerce them to do what you want them to.

When you know that something is true, don't try to appease the other person. Always stand on eternal principles and never yield one iota. You can't appease somebody who's a little Hitler in his or her heart. Appeasement never wins gratitude.

Nobody has power over you. The only influence others can have is that which you give to them in your own mind. You have the freedom to bless or curse them. *To bless* is to say yes to life and to wish for others everything you desire for yourself, including harmony, health, peace, and love.

We're all children of the Most High. Realize this truth, and wonders will unfold in your life. If you repeatedly affirm that you're a child of God, you'll develop a marvelous personality, exude vibrancy, and become flooded with the radiance of limitless light.

Whenever any fear or worry comes to you or whenever you think that you can't accomplish something, get still and quiet and contemplate the sovereignty of Spirit. Realize that Infinite Intelligence is within you and that It is boundless love, eternal life, marvelous wisdom, absolute power, and complete harmony. Nothing can challenge or oppose this God Presence.

Never forget: *You're the master of your soul.* You're in charge of your own conceptive realm—your thoughts, feelings, emotions, and reactions.

⽗⼗⽗ ⽗⼗⽗

Chapter Eight

Handling Injustice

There's no doubt that injustice exists in the world. Life isn't always fair, and we must learn to live with this fact. I've often been asked how we can believe in a God who appears to allow oppression and cruelty to take place, and reward ill doers while punishing good people. I explain that the ways of the Eternal One are unfathomable, and that what appears to be unfair may often be beneficial in the long run. Some ministers comfort people by telling them that they'll receive their reward in heaven. Perhaps this is so, but it's natural to want to enjoy our lives in the here and now.

The law of the subconscious is impersonal and eminently fair at all times. Your deeper mind accepts the impress of your thoughts and reacts accordingly. Your thoughts are seeds, and as you sow, so you reap. If you cultivate orchids, you'll get orchids. You can't plant a crop of evil and expect good to come from it. What you feel, you attract; and what you imagine, you become. That's the law of mind and is absolutely just.

Your mental attitude, not external events or people, determines whether you have success or failure. Your experiences are the exact reproduction of your habitual thoughts and imagery, and you become what you think about all day long.

Don't look for integrity in the world—it isn't there. But you can rise above the mass mind, human spitefulness, and greed by aligning yourself with the principles of right action and justice within you. You need to establish fairness and truth in your own mind.

God is complete justice, pure bliss, boundless love, overflowing joy, absolute order, indescribable beauty, absolute wisdom, and supreme power. And God is the Life Principle *within* you, so stop looking for it elsewhere. Since Spirit is omnipresent, It must be in you— common sense tells you that. When you contemplate the truths of Divine Intelligence, you rise above the injustice and the cruelties of the world and build up a spiritual immunity to the mass mind, which is the thinking of the more than six million people on the planet. Unfortunately, not all of their thoughts are lovely, noble, and godlike.

⇥✛⇤

When Joseph T. came to see me, he was angry, resentful, and bitter about the company he worked for. In the past two years, he'd been passed over for promotion twice. He told me that he'd earned the right to advance through his good work, perfect attendance, and adherence to all company policies and procedures. "I've always received good performance reviews and never—not once—have I been reprimanded," he stated. "When I asked my boss why I didn't get the promotion, he just said that although my work was good, the person who was chosen was better suited for the higher position. I'd quit tomorrow, but jobs are scarce and I can't afford to be unemployed."

I said to Joseph, "You're upset and full of condemnation and criticism for the organization that employs you. These negative suggestions enter your subconscious and result in a loss of promotion, financial increase, and prestige. We promote *ourselves.* Each of us answers our own prayers. Whatever you believe and impress on your conscious mind, the subconscious will bring to pass, whether it's good or bad." I gave him the following mental and spiritual formula to practice daily:

I know that the laws of my mind are absolutely just and that whatever I impress on my subconscious mind is reproduced accurately in my physical world and circumstances. I know that I am using a principle of mind, and a principle is absolutely impersonal. I am equal before the laws of mind, which means that what I truly believe will govern what happens to me.

I instructed him to say this prayer every morning and night. I suggested that before he closed his eyes to sleep, he set his mind on positive thoughts. I said, "Think about the contributions you've made at work, to your family, and in your social and religious activities. Dwell on the compliments you've received from your boss, colleagues, wife, and children. Your dreams will follow these thoughts, and your subconscious will be programmed for success and happiness."

Some months later Joseph reported that he'd been chosen to head up a new department in his company. He told me, "I followed your suggestion, and it not only changed my attitude, it unleashed a stream of creativity I didn't even know I had. When I got this promotion, my supervisor told me that he'd chosen me because the new ideas and suggestions that I'd proposed showed him that I wasn't just a good worker, but an innovator who could meet the challenges of a higher position."

⊰✦⊱

I met an extremely wealthy and philanthropic woman a few years ago. She informed me that she believes that money is like the air around us. She explained, "I came from a family of moderate means, but I always felt that I was rich. After all, I'm God's daughter, and He richly gives me all things to enjoy."

She'd married a young merchant, and together they'd built a successful retail store, which they expanded into a chain. After her husband died, she sold it for millions of dollars and has spent the past few years establishing college scholarships and endowing hospitals and medical clinics in developing countries all around the world. She told me, "Even when I had little money, I always said to myself, 'I am rich and will do good things with my wealth.'"

Whatever you attach to the words *I am,* you become. For example, if you say, "I'm no good"; "I'm a flop"; "I'm a failure"; or "I'm getting old," you will become these things. Therefore, you should affirm: "I am strong, powerful, loving, harmonious, kind, inspired, illumined, and immensely wealthy. I am doing what I love to do and am Divinely happy and prosperous." It's wise to be aware of what you're decreeing when you speak.

Many people who are living in poor circumstances are envious and resentful of the wealth of their neighbors. This mental attitude results in even more lack, limitation, and poverty in their lives. They're unwittingly blocking their own good. They'd have a fortune to share if they'd focus on the truth that they're one with the Infinite Source, for we all have the key that unlocks the treasure-house of the gold mine within.

᚛✠᚜

Shortly after I finished broadcasting one of my lectures, I received a phone call from a listener. He said, "I just heard your talk, and I disagree with you. You said that if I accept that God dwells within me, good things will happen to me. I'm religious man, go to church regularly, and pray daily, but I've experienced nothing but misery. About a year ago, my wife and I left our home-town and moved to Oregon to start a new life. I got a job selling insurance, but have had little success. I live in a poor, rural area. The farmers and small-business owners have little cash, and I just can't make a living. My wife is pregnant, and if I can't turn this situation around, we'll be forced to return to our old town and rely on help from our parents. I want to make it on my own. Why aren't my prayers working for me?"

I suggested that he repeat this spiritual statement:

> *Where I am, God is. The Almighty Source dwells within me and needs me where I am; otherwise, I wouldn't be here. The Divine Presence within me is all-wise, and It knows and sees*

everything. It's the Eternal Life Principle in me, and It reveals to me the next step for attaining the treasures of life. I give thanks for the answer that comes to me as an intuitive feeling or idea that wells up spontaneously from my mind.

He followed my advice and awoke each morning feeling stronger and more confident. Recognizing that the potential to increase his income in his current job was limited, he came up with the idea of capitalizing on his hobby of photography. He bought a camera, took pictures of the beautiful Oregon mountains and valleys, and sold them to travel magazines. He also developed brochures using the gorgeous photos and sent them to travel agencies. Finally, he started a tourism business, which has made him a small fortune. This man has found happiness by tapping into the treasure-house within himself. He discovered his fortune right where he was.

╞╬╡

Diane S. was an environmental engineer with a doctoral degree in her field. From childhood on, she was fascinated by nature and devoted her life to efforts to save the environment. She worked for the Sierra Club researching ways to conserve natural resources. As is often the case in nonprofit fields, her salary was modest. Her sister, on the other hand, had little education, took a job as a showgirl in Las Vegas, and was earning four times as much money as Diane.

Diane said, "It's all so unfair. We need to change the system. I worked extremely hard for six years to get my Ph.D., while my sister never even graduated from high school." I explained to Diane that she could rise above the mass mind, which thinks from the standpoint of circumstances, conditions, and traditions. At my suggestion, she began to practice standing before the mirror each morning and affirming: "Wealth, success, and happiness are mine now."

She repeated this affirmation for about five minutes every morning, knowing that it would impregnate her subconscious. She knew what she was doing and why she was doing it. She realized that she was cultivating the garden of her mind. When you put seeds in the earth and water and fertilize them, they sprout and grow. But you can't *make* a plant blossom—only Infinite Spirit can do that. This Almighty Power is also responsible for manifesting your desires.

After Diane had been saying her prayer for a month, the Sierra Club promoted her to a more important job at a far greater salary. She began to write articles about environmental matters and sell them to magazines, and she signed a book contract with a major publisher.

⊨✦⊨

Millions of people around the world suffer from injustice. Persecution and even genocide still take place. A dictator's greed for power can inflict cruelty on millions of people, and one general's orders can cause hundreds of thousands to suffer. Despots and tyrants have existed down through the ages, and the emulators of Nero, Ivan the Terrible, Hitler, Stalin, and Genghis Khan are still active.

Unfairness exists in homes, factories, jails, and elsewhere. A doctor who's been researching possible cures for cancer for years may earn less than his brother who drives a truck for a living. It doesn't seem quite fair to the doctor, and he's angry about it.

The mothers of the world also work incredibly hard, but they don't belong to any unions or receive a guaranteed wage, and often their children shun them. In my experience, sometimes they're not even invited to their kids' weddings. When I visit senior citizens in rest homes, a common complaint I hear is "My children never come see me."

Justice is based on the golden rule or the law of love. You must become acquainted with this mental and spiritual law in order to be in a position to right the imbalances of the world. The kingdom of heaven where fairness and equality reign is within you. You're a master over your conceptive realm: your thoughts, feelings, actions, and reactions. Paradise is your own mind when it's at peace.

⌖

Millions of people throughout the world are hungry for peace, health, abundance, security, and love. The way to find these things is to get in tune with the Infinite and claim: "Infinite Spirit flows through me as love, harmony, strength, guidance, beauty, and inspiration." This is the bread of life—an intangible but vital form of sustenance. It's the bread of right action, courage, joy, and abundance. How can you live without these qualities?

When you pray: "Give us this day our daily bread," you're asking for that which is your own. God is the Living Spirit within, and the gift has already been given. Therefore, you have to learn to be a receiver, for *all things are ready if the mind be so.*

⌖

Nature is lavish, extravagant, and bountiful. Scientists say that enough fruit rots in the tropics to feed all of humanity. Similarly, there's a boundless spring of ideas, abundance, and love that you can tap into. Infinite Intelligence is within you. You can have an idea that's worth a fortune and provides employment for millions. New concepts about energy or transportation can come to you. You can do wonderful things because the Infinite within reveals ideas to you.

You must persist in taking right action and affirming that which is lovely, noble, and godlike. Continue to have faith, and all good will be yours.

⌖

You'll experience the exact manifestation of your inner beliefs and convictions. As within, so without. As above, so below. As in heaven (meaning your mind), so on earth (your body, environment, conditions, social status, and position in the world).

The wisdom of the Almighty flows through every situation. Adhere to this truth, and when fear arises, affirm: "It is God in action," which means that the Life Principle in you is moving as beauty, harmony, love, and peace. The day will break, and all shadows will disappear.

⌖

According to your belief, your subconscious will respond. For example, the drug amygdalin is used by many people who have cancer. Because the U.S. government bans it, they go down to Mexico to obtain it. It seems unjust to prevent them from trying this potential cure, which is a harmless substance made from apricot seeds. The doctors are saying, "You're going to die, but you must die *our* way." They tell the cancer patients that they're incurable and that it's therefore futile to take amygdalin. However, if these people believe that the drug offers them a chance, why not let them use it? If they believe that it will help, they *will* get results. I've personally known people who claim that they were completely healed of cancer by using amygdalin. The subconscious is a supremely powerful force.

⌖

As we sow, so we reap. There are some who look upon wealth as the air they breathe. They say: "Infinite Intelligence reveals to me wonderful, creative ideas that bless humanity," and new concepts arise in their minds. Many people came to America from other countries. They brought only the clothes on their back, but they had ideas. They studied hard, learned English, and are now running businesses that employ thousands of people. They had faith in the law of mind. You can also achieve great success, because you're a child of the Living God. Therefore, exalt the Divine Spirit in your midst.

※✦※

A man in Los Angeles feared that he would lose his home. He said, "I can't get the money to pay my mortgage. My relatives have turned me down, and the banks won't loan me anything either." He began to dwell on lack, loss, and limitation, and—of course—he lost his home. This is equalization of the inner and the outer. You can't focus on failure and bankruptcy and expect to have prosperity and success. Then the law of mind wouldn't be just. Affirm: "God is the source of my supply. All of my needs are met at every moment." If you have this faith, you'll attract wealth of all kinds— spiritual, mental, and material.

※✦※

The Buddha taught thousands of years ago that ignorance is one of the greatest roadblocks to enlightenment and freedom from suffering. If we're to achieve this blissful state, we must let go of superstition and irrational fears and instead adhere to the law of the subconscious and the power of Infinite Spirit. What we really believe in our heart manifests.

※✦※

We shouldn't take care of people from the cradle to the grave. If we do so, we're psychologically castrating them and robbing them of their Divinity. We're here to make mistakes and discover the Infinite Power within. When we went to school, we had an eraser at the end of our pencil because we're supposed to learn through trial and error. If we coddle people, we deprive them of the chance to learn about themselves and their strengths. We're all children of the Living God and heirs to all that is.

※✦※

A woman was praying for advancement at her job, yet she resented the supervisor, saying to herself, "He's blocking my promotion." I explained to her she was being unjust to herself by placing this man on a pedestal and making him greater than the Infinite within her. Her attitude made no sense, because her desire for promotion, expansion, and growth came from the Life Principle within, which fulfills all wishes. In claiming that the supervisor was greater than Divine Intelligence, she was denying the power of the Infinite, which is omnipotent. That's absurd, isn't it?

I advised her to affirm: "Promotion, advancement, and achievement are mine in Divine law and order, through the power of the Infinite." She used the power of mind to achieve her desire for success at work.

※✛※

There's no such thing as a free lunch in the universe. You have to pay for everything. If you want to become a great singer, you have to go within yourself and say: "God sings majestically through me." You imagine that you're singing in a magnificent way that stirs the souls of your listeners and fills them with peace, happiness, and love. As you continue to repeat this affirmative prayer, you're establishing a mental equivalent that will be manifested in the external world. Of course, you'll still practice your scales and rehearse your scores. You'll have to let your talent and knowledge saturate your subconscious, and then you can play one of Rachmaninoff's preludes blindfolded.

Similarly, if you want to prosper and be successful in life, you have to establish a mental equivalent of wealth in your mind. The Bible says: "With all thy getting, get understanding." Wisdom is an awareness of the presence and power of God within you. You're becoming wise when you know that every thought is creative and manifests itself on the screen of space. If you don't have a healthy respect for your thoughts, you're going to get into lots of trouble.

❄

You can imagine yourself as a bum, and you'll become one. However, you can also envision yourself as a tremendous success. You can visualize yourself as a great actor before an audience, making them laugh and cry. You're realizing the power within you to bring the beauty of Shakespeare alive.

❄

Some of the letters published in newspapers are vitriolic and vindictive. They're written by people filled with self-loathing. When you hate yourself, you project hatred onto others. In fact, it's impossible to hate others unless you first despise yourself. You project how you feel about yourself onto others. It comes out in your speech, art, and everything else.

❄

If your mind exalts the Divine in your husband or wife, then your marriage will grow more blessed and beautiful throughout the years. Why? Because you're seeing the Infinite Intelligence within your spouse. If you dwell on his or her shortcomings, derelictions, and abnormalities (we all have them), then you're reinforcing these states in the other person and also in yourself. You're eating out of the garbage can and are already divorced because you've separated yourself from harmony, peace, love, joy, beauty, kindness, goodwill, and understanding.

Instead, glorify God in your partner and affirm that you're both guided by Infinite Spirit. Divine right action reigns supreme, and your marriage will become stronger and more loving.

❄

You can't gain or lose anything except through your mind. Suppose you told me that you'd lost $30,000 to some con artist who swindled you. Well, it's likely that you didn't investigate him, check with an attorney, or do anything you were supposed to do. You were careless, apathetic, and lazy, and you didn't even use common sense.

You've lost your money, but if you claim that you're now mentally and spiritually identified with the $30,000, it comes back to you in Divine law and order, because whatever you're focused on, your subconscious will magnify and multiply exceedingly. You need to refuse the loss. That's the law of mind. You can't sell a house unless you first sell it mentally, and you can't get a job until you accept one in your mind.

I'm constantly on guard against negative thinking. I cast it out of my mind whenever it enters. I have faith in the Infinite Power and Presence that always works for good. I believe in the goodness and guidance of the Infinite. I open my mind and heart to the influx of the Divine Spirit. I discover an ever-increasing sense of power, wisdom, and understanding. I know the way my subconscious works: It magnifies what I deposit in it. Therefore, my money comes back to me, pressed down, shaken together, and running over. It's God in action.

In a Nutshell

Your inner thoughts, feelings, and imagery determine what you experience in life and make the difference between success and failure.

Whatever you impress on your conscious mind, your subconscious will bring to pass as form, experience, and event. Whatever you really believe with your conscious mind, your subconscious will manifest and magnify, whether it's good or bad.

A great law of mind is this: *Whatever you attach to I am, you become.* For example, if you say, "I'm no good"; "I'm a flop"; "I'm a failure"; or "I'm getting old," you will become these things. Therefore, you should instead say: "I am strong, powerful, loving, harmonious, kind, inspired, illumined, immensely wealthy, and am doing what I love to do. I am Divinely happy."

You must become acquainted with the mental and spiritual laws. Then you'll be in a position to command justice, which means to right imbalances and establish equilibrium. Justice means right thought, feeling, and action, and is based on the golden rule or law of love.

If you want to prosper or be successful in life, you have to establish the mental equivalent of wealth in your mind. The Bible says: "With all thy getting, get understanding." Wisdom is an awareness of the presence and power of God within you. You're becoming wise when you know that your every thought is creative.

☩ ☩

Chapter Nine

---·•·---

The Cure for Hurt Feelings

A while ago, I received a letter from a man who stated that he couldn't understand why everybody around him annoyed him. I asked him to come and see me, and in talking with him, I discovered that he was constantly rubbing others the wrong way. He didn't like himself and was full of self-condemnation. He spoke in a tense, irritable tone that grated on one's nerves. He was also highly critical of himself and others.

I explained to him that although he believed that his unhappy experiences were caused by other people, in fact, his thoughts and feelings about *himself* were the source of his problems. I said that if he despised himself, he couldn't have goodwill and respect for others. It's a law of mind that we're always projecting our thoughts and feelings onto our associates and all those around us.

He began to realize that as long as he projected feelings of prejudice, ill will, and contempt for others, that's exactly what he would get back. I gave him a mental and spiritual formula, which enabled him to overcome his irritation and arrogance. He decided to impress the following thoughts in his subconscious mind:

> *I practice the golden rule from now on, which means that I think, speak, and act toward others as I wish them to think, speak, and act toward me. I walk serenely on my way, and I am free, for I give freedom to all. I sincerely wish peace, prosperity, and success for all. I am always poised, serene, and calm. The*

peace of the Infinite floods my mind and my entire being. Others appreciate and respect me as I appreciate myself. Life is honoring me greatly and providing for me abundantly.

The petty things of life no longer irritate or annoy me. When fear, worry, doubt, or criticism knock at my door, faith, goodness, truth, and beauty respond, and no one is there. The suggestions and statements of others have no power. I know now how to cure hurt feelings. When I think God's thoughts, His power backs me. I know that the thoughts and actions of others have no power unless I give it to them. I am at peace.

He affirmed these truths morning, noon, and night, and he committed the entire prayer to memory. He poured life and love into his words, and these ideas penetrated the layers of his subconscious mind. He was transformed, and he said to me, "I'm getting along with others fine. I've received a promotion at work, and I now know the truth of the passage 'If I be lifted up in my mind, I will draw all manifestation unto me.'"

He realized that his problems were within himself and decided to change his thoughts, feelings, and reactions. Anyone can do the same thing; it requires a decision, stick-to-itiveness, and the keen desire to transform oneself.

Begin to realize that Infinite Intelligence is within you. It controls all of your vital organs and the processes and functions of your body. Your mind is God's mind. Use your imagination and the other great powers of the Divine Presence within you. When you consciously, decisively, and constructively use the Infinite Power within, you become free.

The great American philosopher Emerson wrote about the grandeur and dignity of humankind and encouraged people to expand their concept of themselves and release the infinite possibilities within. He stated: "What Plato has thought, he [everyone] may think; what a saint has felt, he may feel; what at any time has befallen any man, he may understand. He who has access to the universal mind is a party to all that is or can be done, for this is the only and sovereign agent."

Begin to have a lofty, noble, and dignified concept of yourself and the petty aspects of life will no longer irritate you. If they do, you're emotionally immature. That's why people say, "Why don't you act your age?" or "Why don't you grow up?" Are your feathers easily ruffled when someone tells you, "You need to shape up"? Or do you take it in stride and respond, "Well, you're right. I'm going to do better next time"?

Everyone is a child of the Most High. To live a full and happy life, you must live according to principles. When you think, speak, act, and react from the standpoint of the Infinite Intelligence within you, you'll find that your entire life is joyful, successful, and peaceful.

⊫✛⊨

Linda was jealous and hateful toward her office supervisor, Jane. Oh yes, Linda was suffering from hurt feelings and had developed ulcers and high blood pressure. Once she became aware of the spiritual principle of forgiveness and goodwill, she realized that she'd accumulated many resentful feelings that were festering in her subconscious mind. She tried to talk with Jane in an effort to straighten matters out, but the woman brushed her off. In a continuing effort to correct the situation, Linda did affirmative prayer treatment for ten minutes every morning before going to work. She affirmed: "I surround my supervisor with harmony, love, peace, joy, and goodwill."

Now this wasn't mumbo jumbo. She knew what she was doing and why she was doing it. These positive thoughts about her boss sank into her subconscious. Linda also prayed: "There is harmony, peace, and understanding between us. Whenever I think of Jane, I say, 'God's love saturates your being.'" Since there's only one mind, Jane received the benefits of the affirmation.

A few weeks passed, and Linda went on a trip to San Francisco. Upon boarding the plane, she discovered that the only vacant seat was the one next to Jane. Linda greeted her cordially and received a friendly, loving response. They had a wonderful time together in San Francisco. They're now friends and are attending my lectures on Sunday mornings.

Infinite Intelligence worked out a solution to Linda's difficulty that she wouldn't have been able to devise with her conscious mind. In fact, the ways of the subconscious are beyond our understanding. Linda's changed thinking transformed her life and brought about a perfect healing of her ulcers and high blood pressure. She'd been hurting herself with her dark thoughts. Her story illustrates how no one else is responsible for what we think or feel because we're the only thinker in our universe. Only *we* are in charge of what we think about our President, senators, or anybody else.

⚎✛⚎

I recall a young woman saying to me one time, "Everybody in my office hates me, and several people want me to get fired." I asked her why she didn't resign and find another position, and she answered, "What's the use? I've already had three jobs this year."

This woman had a brilliant mind, was well educated, and was an outstanding legal secretary. Most of her problems stemmed from her personality. Did you know that over 90 percent of all of the problems in factories, schools, businesses, and government aren't technical? No, the biggest challenge is people's inability to get along with others. They so often rub each other the wrong way, and their tendency is to blame others.

I gave her a spiritual prescription and suggested that she use it regularly for several months. She repeated the following prayer for every man and woman in her office each day before she went to work:

I send out loving thoughts and feelings of goodwill, happiness, and joy to everyone in my office. I affirm, claim, and believe that my relationship with each of my co-workers is harmonious, pleasant, and satisfactory. Divine love, peace, and beauty flow through my thoughts, words, and deeds, and I am constantly releasing the imprisoned splendor within me. I am happy, free, and bubbling over with enthusiasm. I rejoice in the goodness of God and all people in the land of the living.

She reiterated these truths, and when thoughts of anger or criticism came to her, she poured forth goodwill upon others. Before the end of that year, she received a wonderful promotion and was put in complete charge of the entire legal office.

Anyone who wants to create more harmonious relations can do so. For example, if the thought that you'd like to wring somebody's neck comes to you, what's to prevent you from saying, "God's peace fills your soul"? Nothing! It takes a little practice, but anybody who wants to can do it. How much do you want what you want? Are you willing to give up your grudges, hurt feelings, resentment, and antagonism to achieve good digestion and normal blood pressure? You have to give up something.

∺✛∺

A man recently came to me and said, "I'm all mixed up and can't get along with others. I'm constantly annoying them." This young man was hypersensitive, jittery, self-centered, and grouchy. In spite of all this, he wanted to develop good relationships with his co-workers.

I explained to him that his present personality represented the sum total of his habitual thinking, education, and indoctrination, but that he could transform himself. I told him that the Infinite dwelled within him and that all of the attributes, potencies, and qualities of the Divine were lodged in his deeper mind. They could be resurrected and expressed in his personal life. I gave him the following prayer for the purpose of changing his entire personality. He repeated it feelingly and lovingly several times a day:

> *God is a great personality and the Infinite Life Principle within me. His Presence flows through me now as harmony, joy, peace, love, beauty, and power. I am a channel for the Divine in the same way that a lightbulb is a channel for electricity. The wholeness, beauty, and perfection of the Infinite are constantly being expressed through me. Today I am reborn spiritually. I completely detach myself from my old way of thinking. I bring Divine life, love, truth, and beauty into my experience. I consciously feel love for everyone and radiate goodwill. To everyone I meet, I say mentally, "I see the Divine Presence in you, and I know you see the Divine Presence in me."*
>
> *I recognize the qualities of God in everyone. I practice this morning, noon, and night. It is a living part of me. I am reborn spiritually now, because all day long I practice feeling the presence of the Infinite. No matter what I am doing—whether walking along the street, shopping, or going about my daily business—whenever my mind wanders into worry, criticism, or doubt, I bring it back to the contemplation of the Divine Holy Presence. I feel noble, dignified, and godlike. I sense my oneness with the Infinite, and Its peace fills my soul.*

As this man made a habit of allowing the attributes and qualities of the Infinite Good to flow through his mind, his whole personality underwent a marvelous change. He became more friendly and understanding, and he now radiates vibrancy and goodwill wherever he goes.

The Bible says: "Great peace have those who love Your law, and nothing causes them to stumble." The law is: *I am that which I contemplate and that which I feel myself to be.* With your eyes focused on God, there's no evil on your path. Divine love goes before you today and every day, making your way straight, glorious, and happy. *You will keep him in perfect peace whose mind is stayed on You.*

⧾✛⧾

A husband and wife were quarreling. Both were suffering from hurt pride and were angry. They glowered at each other and shouted. They had a six-year-old daughter who looked at her mom and dad and said, "Both of you deserve a good spanking." Her parents laughed, and the tension was broken. They had to laugh at themselves for being so silly. The whole episode was ludicrous and irrational. They'd been enjoying hurt feelings!

⧾✛⧾

You can't afford hurt feelings because they rob you of everything worthwhile, including vitality, wholeness, beauty, and energy. Resentment is the quickest way in the world to get old, wrinkled, and sick. It leaves you a mental and physical wreck. Nonetheless, some people get a morbid satisfaction out of playing the martyr role. They say, "If you love me, you'll do such and such"; "I will be dead and gone, and you'll be sorry for the way you treated me"; "You're giving me a heart attack"; or "You're killing me now." This is emotional blackmail. They're trying to get you to do what they want you to do. They're certainly not interested in your welfare, happiness, or peace. Instead, they're selfish and possessive. They say, "Do what *I* want you to do."

Do you want all of your relatives and associates to think and believe the way you do? Do you wish that they'd act the way you prefer? Vote the same way? Go to the same church? If you do, you're emotionally immature and haven't grown up. Allow your family and friends to have their freedom and think what they want to think. If they want to believe in a devil, let them do so.

Let them have their peculiarities, eccentricities, and unconventional ways. They have the right to do what they think is best—and so do you.

Your success, prosperity, peace, and happiness aren't dependent upon what others think or don't think, do or don't do, say or don't say, and believe or don't believe. The only thing that matters is what *you* think in your heart, which is your subconscious. As you think and feel, so you are. You're responsible for your thoughts, reactions, and emotions. You're the master of your conceptual realm. The suggestions, statements, and actions of others have no power to disturb you. You can only distress yourself with the thoughts you have about situations. If someone calls you a jerk, you can respond, "Nothing you say can disturb me today. May God's peace fill your soul," and go on about your business. You refuse to give that person the power to give you a headache, upset you, or make a fool out of you. You're too smart for that.

-≕✢≔-

Jealousy wreaks havoc. For example, envious and insecure individuals in the business world are constantly thinking about other people's actions—when they get to work, the prices they're charging, and how they're conducting their business. They don't seem to have any time for their own affairs. It's such a waste of energy, vitality, and enthusiasm.

Do you think that the person you're jealous of blocks your good? No, it's your own thoughts and beliefs that are limiting you. If you covet somebody's talents and possessions, you feel inferior and are full of fear. You're placing the other person on a pedestal and saying, "You're way up there, and I'm down here." You're demoting yourself and are certainly attracting lack and limitation in every area of your life. It's disastrous.

-≕✢≔-

Awhile ago I had a consultation with a member of my congregation. He said that he was shy and resentful and viewed the world as harsh and cruel. He felt that people didn't appreciate him and looked down on him. He had an inner sense of inadequacy and was critical of himself. He asked me, "How can I gain the respect of others?"

I gave him a biblical quotation: "Love your neighbor as yourself." The real meaning of this passage is that your neighbor *is* you, and your real self is the Divine Presence within you.

I explained to this young man that if he despised himself, he couldn't gain the esteem of other people, for it's a cosmic law of mind that we constantly project our thoughts, feelings, and beliefs onto others. What we send out comes back to us. If we're mean and cruel to ourselves, others are going to be mean and cruel to us.

⌖

You're a child of the Infinite, and all the powers and qualities of God are within you. You must love and honor the Indwelling Presence. To love yourself is to recognize and honor the Living Spirit within you. The Supreme Intelligence made, created, and sustains you. It's the Life Principle.

This has nothing to do with egotism or self-aggrandizement; on the contrary, it's a wholesome veneration of the Divinity that shapes your destiny. The Bible says that your body is a temple of the Infinite and that you're here to glorify God. When you respect and love yourself, you'll automatically esteem and care for others.

Love the *I am* within you. When you say "I am," you're announcing the Presence of the Living God inside you. It's the Spirit in you that created you. It's all-wise and sees all. Surely you should honor this Infinite Intelligence. That's the real meaning of loving your neighbor as yourself.

In A Nutshell

Begin to realize that Divine Intelligence, the Guiding Principle of the universe, is within you. The Infinite Healing Presence controls all of your vital organs and the processes and functions of your body. Your mind is actually God's mind. Use your imagination and the many other powers you possess. When you consciously, decisively, and constructively tap into the Infinite Power within, you become free.

No one else is responsible for how you think and feel—*you* are, because you're the only thinker in your universe. You're in charge of what you think about your President, senators, or anybody else.

Great peace have they who love thy law, and nothing shall offend them. And the law is: *I am that which I contemplate; I am that which I feel myself to be.* With your eyes fixed on God, there's no evil on your path. Divine love goes before you today and every day, making your way straight, glorious, and happy.

You can't afford to have hurt feelings because they rob you of everything worthwhile. Resentment is the quickest way in the world to get old, wrinkled, and sick. Feeling wounded takes away your vitality, enthusiasm, energy, and good discernment. It leaves you a mental and physical wreck.

The only thing that matters is what you believe in your heart, which is your subconscious. As you think and feel, so you are. You're responsible for your reactions, thoughts, and feelings. The suggestions, statements, and actions of others have no power to disturb you. You can only distress yourself with your own thoughts about situations.

Learn to love your true self, and then you'll be able to respect and care about others.

Chapter Ten

---·•·---

Handling Difficult People

On the islands of Hawaii, you find people from many ethnic groups and with diverse religious beliefs living together peacefully and enjoying the sunshine of God's love. On one of my visits to the islands, the Hawaiian who drove me from the airport to my hotel told me that his heritage was a mixture of Irish, Portuguese, German, Japanese, and Chinese. He pointed out that the people who live in Hawaii have intermarried for generations and that racial conflict is unknown.

It's so important to have harmonious relationships. One of the chief reasons why some men and women don't get ahead in life is their inability to get along with others. But the trouble really is within themselves. They're frustrated and they project their animosity onto others, often failing to realize their own dreams and aspirations.

The best way to get along with others is to salute the Divinity in them and realize that we're all a manifestation of God. There's only one Celestial Father, the common progenitor of humankind. We're all intimately related, and every person who walks the earth is a son or daughter of the Infinite Intelligence. Therefore, to hurt another is to hurt ourselves. Perhaps in stupidity we don't realize this, but it's nevertheless absolutely true. As well, when we respect and honor the Divinity within ourselves, we'll automatically honor the Divinity in other people.

✠

Love your neighbor as yourself. People are confused about this biblical quotation. They ask, "How can I love that fellow? He beats his wife, comes home drunk, and is mean to his children." Love has nothing at all to do with this—not a thing in the world. *Love* in the Bible isn't a sentiment or emotion; it means that you have a healthy reverence for the Divinity that created you, started your heartbeat, grew the hair on your head, and gave you the whole world when you were born. Everything you needed was here, including the air, sunshine, and water.

Now if you don't have a wholesome reverence for the Eternal Intelligence, how on earth can you respect the Divinity in anybody else? You can't. But when you honor the Infinite Spirit within, It answers your prayers. And when you revere God in yourself, you'll automatically respect Him in others, too. This is what it means to love your neighbor as yourself.

If you don't respect the Divine within, you can't honor it in others. That's why a man can't love his wife, children, or anybody else unless he first loves himself, for his essence is God, the Living Spirit that created him. To love is to give your allegiance and loyalty to the One Source. If you're giving power to the stars, the sun, the moon, the weather, strawberries, or anything else, then you're devoting yourself to a created thing, not the *Creator.*

In the Ten Commandments, it says: "Thou shalt have no other gods before me . . . . for I, the Lord thy God, am a jealous god," This passage means that you shouldn't have loyalty to anything other than the One Power. It moves as unity and harmony, and nothing can oppose, thwart, or vitiate it. Therefore, you need to recognize and honor the Divine Presence. Don't place someone on a pedestal and say, "This person can block my good." Then you're giving power to something other than God and are being unjust to yourself.

⚜

When visiting one of the hotels in Hawaii, I had an interesting conversation with a waiter named Tony. He told me that every year, an eccentric millionaire from the mainland visited the hotel. This visitor proved to be a miserly type who hated to give waiters or bellboys a tip. He was churlish, rude, and just plain ornery. Nothing satisfied him. He was constantly complaining about the food and the service, and snarled at the restaurant staff whenever he was served. Tony said to me, "I realized that he was a sick man. A kahuna (a native Hawaiian shaman) says that when people are like that, there's something eating them inside. So I decided to treat him with kindness."

Tony consistently treated the surly man with courtesy, generosity, and respect, silently affirming: "God loves and cares for him. I see the Divine in him, and he sees the Divine in me." He practiced this technique for about a month, at the end of which time this eccentric millionaire said, "Tony, you're the best waiter I've ever had."

Tony told me, "I almost fainted. I expected a growl and got a compliment. He gave me $500 as a parting tip."

This waiter had addressed his thoughts to the soul (subconscious mind) of the cantankerous guest. They gradually melted the ice in the man's heart, and he responded in love and kindness. Tony proved that seeing the Presence of God in the other and adhering to the great Eternal Truth pays fabulous dividends in human relations—spiritually as well as materially.

⚜

I had an interesting conversation with a social director, Marie, in one of the hotels on Maui. She remarked that sometimes when she says to a guest, "It's a wonderful day," the guest mutters, "What's good about it? I hate the weather here, and I don't like anything about this place."

Marie stated that she knew that people with such sour attitudes were emotionally disturbed and driven by some irrational emotion. She'd studied psychology at the university in Honolulu and remembered that her instructor had noted that we don't resent or get angry at someone because he can't use his legs or suffers from an obvious congenital deformity. Instead, we usually have compassion for the person. Similarly, her teacher said, we shouldn't get upset because some people are emotionally ill and have twisted, warped mentalities. We need to try to understand their disturbed mental state and offer them empathy and understanding.

Marie is gracious, charming, and amiable. Nobody can ruffle her feathers because she's built up a kind of Divine immunity. She fully realizes that no one can hurt her but herself; that is, she has the freedom—as we all do—to bless or resent the people she meets. She can choose her reaction to the situations that arise in her life, and the movement of her thought is under her complete control.

The suggestions, statements, and actions of other individuals have no power to disturb you. It's your own thoughts about circumstances and people that can cause you distress. You can say, "God is guiding me now and peace fills my soul" or "He's a scoundrel and is driving me crazy." *You* generate the peace or the anger. You're the boss and are in control. No one else has any real power to bother you.

※✛※

A young musician who plays the violin at night to pay for his law studies told me that he'd experienced conflict with some of his professors and that his memory had failed him during his oral and written examinations. He was tense and resentful.

I explained to him that his subconscious contains a perfect memory of everything he's read and heard, but that when his conscious mind is tense, the wisdom of the subconscious is blocked. I gave him a spiritual treatment to practice every morning and night: "The Infinite Intelligence in my subconscious mind reveals to me everything I need to know, and I am Divinely guided in my studies. I radiate love and goodwill to my teachers, and I am at peace with them. I pass all of my examinations in Divine order."

He impressed these thoughts on his subconscious, since whatever we plant in our deeper mind will come to pass in Divine order. That's the way we learned to walk, swim, dance, and drive a car. We repeated a thought pattern and an act over and over again. After some time, the action became "second nature," which is the response of our subconscious mind to our conscious thinking and acting. It's automatic and compulsive. It's called *prayer*.

Three weeks went by, and I received a letter from the man saying he'd passed a special examination with flying colors and that his relationships with his professors were now excellent. He succeeded in incorporating into his subconscious mind the idea of perfect memory and harmonious relations with his instructors. His emanation of love and goodwill was subconsciously picked up by his teachers, resulting in strong rapport and communication.

♯✦♯

There's a volcano in Hawaii called Haleakala. Although it hasn't erupted in several hundred years, scientists predict that it will erupt again in the future. I visited Haleakala with a group of people that included an Australian doctor and his wife. He told me that his habit of judging people too harshly had wreaked havoc in his life that was as bad as the damage caused by a volcanic eruption. He said that he used to boil over with rage at what columnists wrote in the newspaper. He sent vindictive, angry letters to members of parliament, the heads of various unions, and others. This internal seething and turmoil had brought on three physical eruptions in his body in the form of two severe cardiac attacks and a mild stroke.

While he was in the hospital after his second heart attack, a nurse gave him the 23rd and 91st Psalms to read, saying: "Doctor, this is wonderful medicine." He began to dwell upon the 23rd Psalm:

The Lord is my Shepherd; I shall not want.
He makes me to lie down in green pastures; He leads me
    beside the still waters.
He restores my soul . . . .
Yea, though I walk through the valley of the shadow of death,
    I will fear no evil;
    for You are with me; Your rod and Your staff, they
    comfort me . . . .
Surely goodness and mercy shall follow me all the days of
my life;
And I will dwell in the house of the Lord Forever.

He also contemplated the inner meaning of the 91st Psalm:

He who dwells in the secret place of the Most High shall abide
    under the shadow
    of the Almighty.
I will say of the Lord, "He is my refuge and my fortress;
    My God, in Him I will trust." . . . .
He shall cover you with His feathers, and under His wings you
    shall take refuge . . .

As the Australian doctor focused on these psalms, their meaning gradually sank into his soul, and he became more compassionate and lost his judgmental attitude. He became healthy and realized that he'd brought his problems upon himself. He said that he learned to accept people, realizing that they're all conditioned differently and that this is a world of imperfect human beings striving toward perfection. He also learned to be true to the God within and respect the Divinity in others.

It's impossible to dwell upon the great eternal truths that have stood the test of time for thousands of years and not develop a peaceful mind. People down through the ages have used these psalms in cases of shipwreck, fire, emergencies, so-called incurable diseases, and all manner of trouble. These holy words have protected them. They're written in the universal, subjective mind that the Hindus call the *Akashic Records*. Therefore, as you use these psalms, even if you don't understand their inner meaning, you're tapping into the experiences and healings of others throughout history. You'll get a response, and marvelous results will follow.

Shakespeare said, "To thine own self be true, and it must follow, as the night the day, thou canst not then be false to any man." The Australian doctor had learned that to understand all is to forgive all. He's still intolerant of false ideas, but not hostile to people. He remains true to the eternal principles of God.

·✠·

A man with whom I went swimming in the beautiful ocean of Maui said to me, "I'm here to get away from it all." Then he began to criticize everybody in his organization, as well as the government. He even seemed to have a grudge against the Infinite. In fact, he told me that he felt that his life would be better if God would just leave him alone. He asked me, "What can I do to have better relationships and get along with these ugly, nasty people?"

I told him that research has demonstrated that one of the major sources of difficulty that many people have in their relationships is that they don't look within themselves for the cause of problems. I pointed out to him that much of his trouble with his employees and associates came primarily from himself and that these other people might be considered secondary causes. He admitted that he was full of hidden rage and was deeply frustrated in his ambitions and plans in life.

He began to see that his suppressed anger kindled the latent hostility in those around him and that *he* provoked the very reactions from others that bothered him so much. He discovered that what he thought was the animosity and irate behavior of his co-workers and clients was actually his own. I gave him a spiritual affirmation, which he was to repeat regularly and systematically:

I know that there is a law of cause and effect and that the mood that I generate is returned to me in the reactions of people and in conditions and events. I realize that my inner turmoil and anger set off ugliness and anger in men, women, and animals. I think, speak, and act from the Divine Center within me. I radiate love, peace, and goodwill to everyone around me and to all people everywhere. The Infinite Being lies stretched in smiling repose within me. Peace is the power at the heart of God; and His river of harmony floods my mind, heart, and whole being. I am one with the Infinite peace of God.

My mind is part of the Infinite mind. What's true of the Infinite is true of me. I realize and know that no person, place, or thing in the entire world has the power to upset, annoy, or disturb me without my mental consent. My thought is creative, and I consciously and knowingly reject all negative thoughts and suggestions, affirming that God is my guide and watches over me. I know that Infinite Intelligence is my real employer, and I am working for this Presence and Power that animates and sustains me. My real self is God, the Living Spirit within me. It cannot be hurt, vitiated, or thwarted. I send kindness, love, and joy to all people; and I know that goodness, truth, and beauty follow me all the days of my life, for I live in the house of the Infinite forever.

After he spent three weeks repeating the above affirmation, he told me that this spiritual practice had replaced his chaotic state of mind with serenity and a sense of imperturbability. Peace is the power at the heart of God, and in the depths of yourself is absolute bliss and harmony.

⊟✛⊟

I had an interesting conversation with Toru, a Japanese businessman who philosophized: "I've been in business for 50 years and have traveled extensively. I've learned that people are basically good and honest, and I take them as they come. They've all had different training and conditioning and have diverse customs and religious beliefs. I know that complaining about these people and getting angry with customers won't change them, so I don't let them disturb me. I refuse to let anybody get under my skin. I bless them all and walk on."

Toru showed me a list of ten customers who'd owed him considerable sums of money and had ignored several bills he'd sent them. He said, "I've been praying for each one morning and night, realizing that the Infinite Presence is prospering them in every way and that It guides, directs, and multiplies their good. I pray that they pay their bills gladly and that they're honest, sincere, and blessed in all their ways. I started doing this a month ago, and eight of my customers have paid and apologized for the delay. There are two to go, but I know that they'll pay, too."

He discovered that when he changed his mental attitude toward the delinquent customers, they also changed. You should also treat people with respect and honor the Divinity within them. God is within everyone. Maybe they're cutthroats or criminals, but they have the Holy Presence within. It may be dormant or asleep, but It's always there. It's in your husband, wife, children, and everyone you meet.

⌖

Radiate love and goodwill to everyone. It costs nothing and pays fabulous dividends. Realize that nobody who's well adjusted acts in a contentious, surly manner. If you have difficult people in your life, surrender them to the Infinite and declare your freedom. Say: "I surrender them to God, who takes them out of my life in Divine law and order. And this same Presence and Power takes me out of their lives in Divine law and order." And so it will be. It will be as if the earth swallowed them up. You'll find yourself in green pastures and beside still waters.

We meet people everywhere—in the office, while shopping, or when we travel. We must learn to get along with them. There are more than six billion individuals in the world today, and the population is increasing every day. There's no point in getting angry with them or becoming a recluse, for any problems you encounter are within *you,* and you can't run away from yourself. If you have a nasty and ugly disposition, you'll attract unpleasant people, for like attracts like. You'll draw them to you wherever you go.

⁜

If we practiced the golden rule and the law of love, we wouldn't need any utopias or gardens of Eden or things of that nature. It would be heaven on earth. If we treated others as we'd like to be treated, there would be no occasion for war, sickness, or disease. We wouldn't need any armed forces or nuclear weapons. It's as simple as that.

The great law of love has been taught for thousands of years, but people act according to their conditioning, fears, hates, and prejudices. If they're governed by ignorance, this produces strife and suffering. When Buddha was meditating, he asked the God Presence what caused all the suffering and crime in India. The answer he received was *ignorance,* which is the only sin. Therefore, it's important to teach people about the unlimited ability to go within to the Divine and claim guidance, inspiration, wealth, prosperity, and success. Then they won't want to hurt anybody in the world, because they'll have found the Source within themselves. Knowledge of the laws of mind and the way of the Spirit will produce health, happiness, peace, abundance, and security.

⁜

Bruce, a sales representative for a pharmaceutical company, went to see a doctor to give a presentation about a new drug his company had developed. The doctor was a friend of his, and they frequently played golf and cards together. However, the doctor was very insulting, criticized Bruce and his presentation, and denigrated the pharmaceutical industry. The salesman was aghast and disturbed. However, a nurse said, "Don't pay any attention to him this morning. His only son died on the operating table last night." Instantly Bruce understood and had compassion for the doctor instead of anger.

Notice how irritation and inner disturbance drop away when we hear about the sorrow and tragedy that another person suffers. The heart melts and love takes over. To understand all is to forgive all.

⌘

A few years ago I read about a woman who'd called the police and said that her husband had threatened her with a gun. Several officers arrived, but no gun was found in the house. What had really happened was that the couple had gotten into a big fight, and the wife had become so angry that she called the police and lied. She was very sorry and regretted it, but the damage had been done. The newspapers publicized the story, and the man's reputation was ruined. This is what irrational emotion does. Negative feelings compel you to act them out. When you want to be nice, you're ugly; when you want to succeed, you fail.

Many people become victims of their own irrational emotions. The solution is to ask yourself: *Is this Infinite Intelligence and Divine Love thinking, speaking, and acting through me?* If not, stop and tune in to the Holy Presence, your guide and counselor. Affirm to yourself:

This Presence is Infinite Peace and Absolute Harmony. Its peace fills my soul. I dwell in the Secret Place of the Most High. I abide in the shadow of the Almighty. I will say of the Lord, He is my refuge, my fortress, my God; in Him will I trust. Here I dwell beyond time and space. Here I am in tune with the Infinite, which lies stretched in smiling repose. I know that to be alone in the silence is to be alone with God. No one can lay siege to me there.

This Divine contemplation supplants all negative thoughts and emotions and heals you.

❈

People fight over their religious beliefs in many parts of the world today, as you know. For example, an American went over to Northern Ireland and spent some months there. When he came back, he was asked what it was like. "Well," he said, "the Catholics and the Protestants hate each other. Little boys of seven are throwing stones at Catholic soldiers, and little girls are also learning to toss grenades at Protestants. It's frightening. I wish they were all heathens so that they might live together like Christians."

Of course, there's some humor in his statement, but he's pointing out the problem of negative conditioning. Muslims, Hindus, Christians, and people of various other religious beliefs have been fighting each other down through the ages. But true spiritual belief should give you joy, peace, and happiness. For in Him there's fullness of joy and no darkness at all. The fruits of the spirit are love, joy, peace, gentleness, goodness, and faith. These are the powers within you. Therefore, you have a wonderful opportunity to radiate love, peace, and goodwill to all humankind. It costs you nothing and pays fabulous dividends. When a God of love is enthroned in your mind, it dominates all other thoughts, feelings, beliefs, actions, and reactions. That's the ideal religion.

❈

The Bible says: "Do not judge, or you too will be judged. For in the same way you judge others, you will be judged, and with the measure you use, it will be measured to you." All of us can avoid mental pain, anxiety, and tension by ceasing to pass judgment in our minds. As Marcus Aurelius said 2,000 years ago: "Where there is no opinion, there is no suffering; where there is no judgment, there is no pain." You're the cause of your own misery. If you get upset about what some politician says or does, who's suffering? You are! Of course, you know that you're provoking your own pain with your judgments and thoughts. Let your opinion be still. If the cucumber is bitter, don't eat it. If there are briars or brambles on the road, avoid them. If there's no judgment, there's no suffering.

You could get agitated about what a senator or the President says, but you should be spiritually mature and realize that people have freedom of speech. You also have the freedom to disagree and write a constructive letter to them telling them what you think and believe. You can do this in a constructive way, but if you get angry and are looking for trouble, you're the one who suffers.

⋇

Don't try to puncture the egos of other people—there's no point in deflating them. Maybe their ideas are foolish, but all you'll do is generate hostility. You could say, "Your idea is interesting and it should be explored further." You're respecting others, and they'll in all probability show you some respect in return. We're all sons and daughters of the Most High and children of Eternity, so don't ride roughshod over people and say, "I believe it, and therefore you should, too" or "This is my opinion, and you must share it." No, you show respect for everyone. You just state what you think, but you don't ridicule others. All that does is cause resentment and antagonism. It doesn't do you or anyone else any good.

⋇

A husband used to come home and criticize his wife, finding fault with her hair, the dinner she made, and the way she was bringing up the children. She began to cry copiously, and the tears brought satisfaction to him, because he was sadistic. I told the wife, "You'd better wake up. Tell your husband that he no longer can disturb you with his remarks. Say, 'I'm on to your game. Your criticism can no longer bother me. I go within to the Infinite, which is my guide and counselor. I'm going to sing a hymn. I'm going to vacuum the floor or take a walk. I'm going to tune in to the Eternal One living in the hearts of all people.'"

It wasn't what her husband said that caused her distress; it was her thoughts about it. The suggestions, statements, and actions of others have no power to disturb us. It's the movement of our own thought that always determines how we feel.

⊨✠⊨

Some people enjoy being hurt by others. A woman in London was regularly beaten up by her husband. He'd come home drunk and abuse her. Finally, he hurt her so much that he was arrested. In court, the judge said to the wife, "Have you anything to say before we pronounce a sentence on your husband?"

She said, "Oh, your Honor . . . I love him so much!"

The judge replied, "Madam, you don't know what love is. England doesn't love him. He gets three years in jail."

The poor woman hated herself and wanted someone to punish her. That's wrong. Love doesn't do anything unloving. It's the Spirit of God. If you love someone, you want to see that person be happy, joyous, and free. You don't do anything mean or criticize, and you certainly don't beat your loved one. Love is of God, and God is love. When you cherish another, you see the Infinite Presence in him or her. You say to yourself, "What's true of God is true of that person."

Nonetheless, some people like to needle others and go out of their way to make cutting remarks or embarrass them. Why do they do this? You must realize that they're frustrated, have an inferiority complex, and feel inadequate. They get a morbid satisfaction out of hurting others. But you can't be hurt. You say: "God dwells within me and walks and talks in me. God is my guide." Then you're immunized, and they can't hurt you.

᛭✝᛭

Think of the many people who've served humanity, including Abraham Lincoln, Winston Churchill, Thomas Edison, Clara Barton, and Helen Keller. We honor all of them and build monuments to them because they contributed so much to people. You can also radiate love, peace, and goodwill to everyone. You get what you expect, so expect guidance, harmony, health, peace, joy, abundance, security, and all the riches of the Infinite. You'll experience marvelous and wonderful unfoldings, for all things are ready if the mind be so.

Live in the joyous expectancy of the best. Release everyone to God and wish for them health, happiness, peace, and all the blessings of heaven. Realize that Infinite Intelligence guides and directs you in all your ways. It's a light upon your path. Divine law and order govern your life, and peace fills your soul.

If you're dealing with difficult people, say: "I release them all [mention their names] to the Infinite that created them. This God Presence takes them out of my life and takes me out of their life in Divine order and through Divine love."

The Bible says: "Whatever things you ask when you pray, believe that you receive them, and you will have them." If you can believe, all things are possible. Believe in the goodness of God in the land of the living; the guidance and riches of the Infinite; and a Divine Spirit that loves, watches over, and strengthens you. All of your ways will then be pleasant, and your paths will be peaceful.

In a Nutshell

When you honor the Infinite Spirit that watches over you, It answers your prayers. When you respect and honor this Divine Presence in yourself, you'll automatically respect It in others. If you disregard the Divine within, you can't honor It in others and will suffer from disharmonious relationships.

Peace is the power at the heart of God. The Infinite lies stretched in smiling repose. The finite is your own conscious mind, where all the trouble is, but in the depths of yourself is absolute bliss and harmony.

Radiate love and goodwill to all. It costs nothing—and it pays fabulous dividends. Realize that nobody who's well adjusted acts in a hostile, antagonistic way.

Ignorance is the only sin. On the other hand, knowledge of the laws of mind and the way of God will produce health, happiness, peace, abundance, and security.

True religion gives you joy. When a God of love is enthroned in your mind, it dominates all other thoughts, feelings, beliefs, actions, and reactions. That's the ideal religion. The fruits of that spirit are love, joy, peace, gentleness, goodness, and faith.

If you're dealing with difficult people, say: "I release them all [mention their names] to the Infinite that created them. This God Presence takes them out of my life and takes me out of their life in Divine order and through Divine love."

Believe in the goodness of God in the land of the living; the guidance and riches of the Infinite; and a Divine Spirit that loves, watches over, and strengthens you. According to your belief, it's done unto you.

⛧ ⛧

Chapter Eleven

Jonathan Livingston Seagull: A Spiritual Interpretation

Some years ago, a novella called *Jonathan Livingston Seagull* was written by Richard Bach and became one of the best-selling books of its time. Jonathan was a seagull who didn't want to be just one of the flock, screeching and diving for old scraps of fish. He realized that there was something grander and greater that he could accomplish, and he wanted to learn to become extremely skilled at flying.

His mother asked, "Why is it so hard for you to be like the rest of the seagulls?"

Jonathan replied, "Mom, I just want to know what I can do in the air and what I can't. That's all. I just want to know."

Jonathan persisted in his dream, but his father said to him, "Winter isn't far away. There won't be many boats out, and the fish will be swimming deep in the ocean. If you must study, then study how to get food. This flying business is all very well, but it doesn't provide you with sustenance. Don't forget that the reason we fly is to eat."

Jonathan nodded obediently. For the next few days he tried to behave like the other gulls the way his parents wanted him to, screeching and fighting for fish. But his heart wasn't in it. *It's all so silly and pointless,* he thought. *I could be spending all that time practicing to fly faster and higher . . . there's so much to learn.*

He continued to work to improve his flying capacity. He suffered many setbacks but found a way to fly faster than any other seagull had ever flown, finally reaching a speed of over 100 miles per hour. After this breakthrough, he thought that the other gulls would be delighted and honor him, but the elders in the flock told him that he'd violated the dignity and traditions of the gull family and banished him from society to lead a solitary life on the far cliffs.

"One day, Jonathan Livingston Seagull, you shall learn that irresponsibility doesn't pay," said the leader of the elders. "We're put in this world to eat and stay alive as long as we possibly can."

A seagull never speaks back to the flock council, but Jonathan's voice rose. "Irresponsibility, my brothers!?" he cried. "Who's more responsible than a gull who finds and follows a meaning . . . a higher purpose in life? For thousands of years we've scrambled after fish, but now we have a better reason to live, discover, and be free. Give me a chance. Let me show you about the new life and what I've learned."

The flock might as well have been stone. The gulls solemnly closed their ears and turned their backs on him, and Jonathan was exiled to the far cliffs.

After he'd been there for a while, two gulls appeared, streaking down in flawless formation. They said to him, "We've come to take you home." A home is with God, the Secret Place of the Most High where you abide in the shadow of the Almighty.

He went with the gulls to a higher plane of existence and met many other birds who shared his love of flying. He also met the wisest seagull, Chiang, who taught him how to transport himself instantly to any place in the world by overcoming the limits of the three-dimensional body. Jonathan learned that heaven was within himself and that the most important thing is to reach out for perfection.

⊱✦⊰

A bird has two wings, which are symbolic of thought and feeling. These are the Divine agencies that move, fashion, and control your entire future. Every thought that's felt as true or "emotionalized" is embodied in the subconscious and comes forth as experiences, conditions, and events in your life. That's the law of mind. It's immutable and timeless. It's just as true as any law of science.

All of us have the wings of imagination and faith, which enable us to soar above problems and contemplate the way things ought to be. We can focus on the Divine solution and a happy ending, knowing that the answer is already within that Supreme Intelligence that lives in all people.

The Bible says: "I bore you on eagles' wings and brought you to Myself." When there's a monsoon, typhoon, hurricane, or storm of any kind, an eagle soars above it and remains poised and calm. When the bad weather abates, the eagle returns to the earth. This noble bird is a national symbol of the United States, chosen to remind us that when we're suffering from difficulties, confusion, or sickness, we can turn to God within and contemplate the harmony, health, peace, joy, and inspiration that come down from heaven. This is why the Bible says: "Give us this day our daily bread." The passage is referring to the bread of peace, happiness, wisdom, and inspiration. We're fed by these things; and we'll never be hungry for goodness, truth, and beauty if we contemplate the God Presence within, calling upon It to guide and direct us. We can turn to the Divine and claim right action, beauty, love, peace, and abundance.

When the eagle is hungry, it flies off to a place where there's food. Its environment doesn't limit it. As transcendental beings, we're also not limited by our surroundings or external conditions. In prayer therapy, we're taught to lift our consciousness *above* the problem. We only need to move our focus from the difficulty and concentrate gently on the Infinite Presence and Power, which knows only the answer. As we rise to a higher state of consciousness, the solution will come. *Before they call, I will answer; And while they are still speaking, I will hear.*

※✦※

In learning to fly faster than any seagull ever had, Jonathan Livingston Seagull stumbled and fell many times. Well, failures are stepping-stones for your climb to success. When you went to school, there was an eraser on the end of your pencil because everyone knew that you'd make mistakes. But through your errors, you grew, advanced, and moved forward in the light. These so-called failures aren't actually a problem: They pave the way to your triumph. So Jonathan was unashamed. He stretched his wings and decided to try and try again. More than anything else, he loved to fly.

Remember that one success wipes out all previous defeats. For example, Thomas Edison made hundreds of attempts before he created the long-lasting, incandescent lightbulb. He finally accomplished his goal. Were all of his previous tries failures? No—he'd simply found numerous methods that didn't work and that he didn't have to try again. They were stepping-stones to his achievement.

Like Jonathan and Edison, you can learn to fly to the higher dimensions of your mind. If you love mathematics, it will reveal its secrets to you. If you're enthralled by music, you'll excel and become a great musician. As you begin to love and give your attention, devotion, and loyalty to the Divine Presence within, you'll soar above problems and become a master in your field of endeavor. You won't be just one of the flock or herd.

※✦※

The nature of Infinite Intelligence is responsiveness. There are many people who solve the most difficult problems by affirming feelingly, knowingly, and lovingly: "God's love fills my soul. God is guiding me now, revealing to me everything I need to know at all times everywhere." Gradually, the realization of Divine love saturates your entire being. Fill your subconscious with life-giving patterns and eradicate the negative ones. As you do this, you'll empty your mind of everything that's unlike God.

Your subconscious is controlled by your conscious mind, which is like the captain of a ship: He or she gives orders to the crew in the engine room, and they carry them out—no matter what. They don't talk back to the captain. The deeper mind is amenable to any suggestions and directions you give to it. What orders are *you* giving to your subconscious mind?

⇥✦⇤

The garden of Eden is an allegory. Your subconscious is the garden and your conscious mind is the gardener. If you cultivate thoughts of harmony, health, beauty, love, right action, inspiration, and guidance, you'll have a wonderful garden full of the most gorgeous flowers. What you sow in your subconscious, so also will you reap. After all, it's the nature of the apple seed to become an apple tree. What are you planting in your garden right now?

If you wish for health, you must give your attention, devotion, and loyalty to the Healing Presence within, realizing that It created you, sustains you, and knows all the processes and functions of your body. Therefore, claim that this miraculous Power is healing, restoring, and transforming your entire being. When you go to a doctor, bless her, realizing that she's guided by Divine Intelligence to facilitate your perfect health.

⇥✦⇤

Just as Jonathan refused to give up his dream, you must not give up yours. You're here to rise above the crowd and grow. You aren't here to conform. Everyone is unique, with different fingerprints, nervous systems, and dreams. You're entirely different from any other person in the world because God never repeats Himself. Therefore, why on earth should you go along with everyone else's ideas?

If you're mired in the mud of life, nobody pays any attention to you. But when you put your head above the crowd, people may throw stones or take potshots at you. Emerson wrote that when you're a nonconformist, the world attacks you. However, who wants to conform? All of the great achievers of the world—whether they were scientists, artists, religious leaders, or inventors—were unorthodox thinkers. These are the people who contributed to humanity, including Louis Pasteur, Sir Isaac Newton, George Washington Carver, Guglielmo Marconi, Thomas Edison, and Albert Einstein. Einstein didn't conform to the mechanistic beliefs that prevailed in his time. On the contrary, he knew that this world consists of energy and frequencies and is alive and dynamic.

George Washington Carver was a slave who carried his master's books, but he had a vision. He wanted to be educated and become a scientist—and he became an innovative botanist and invented hundreds of uses for the peanut and other plants. He's honored by the world today.

Guglielmo Marconi decided to explore the mysterious energy waves that we can't see but that are all around us. Do you know what his relatives did to him? They put him in a straitjacket for six weeks. They said that he was insane. Nevertheless, he made major contributions to the development of radio communication.

Thomas Edison was sent home from school. The teachers said that he was stupid and couldn't learn. But his mother—and Edison himself—didn't agree. He decided to light up the world and invented the lightbulb and many other things.

⊨✦⊨

Note that Jonathan never stopped trying to improve his flying skills. If you persevere, you'll also succeed. The first astronauts who tried to get to the moon suffered many setbacks, but they maintained their vision and ultimately triumphed. These failures were stepping-stones to their success. After all, the joy is in overcoming—that's the way you sharpen your mental and spiritual tools and get ahead in life. If you've had some disappointments, don't look upon them as defeats. Unfortunately, when some people are faced with failure or disappointment, they want to end it all. They despair and think, *What's the use? I'm at the end of my rope.* They sometimes even contemplate suicide. They may be at the bottom, but now the only way to go is up. *Turn your eyes to the hills from whence cometh your help.* The hills, of course, represent the God Presence within.

People with a suicidal complex are looking for a solution. They want freedom, but if they jump off a bridge, they don't solve their problems. You can't overcome any difficulties by running away from them because you carry your mind with you wherever you go. The problem is in your mind, and that's where you need to solve it. You're not your body—you're a transcendental being. You're not limited by your physical self.

⇥✛⇤

Although Jonathan told his parents that he'd stop pursuing his dream of flying, he couldn't keep that promise. However, it's better to break a bad promise than to keep it. For example, some ministers preach that a marriage is a commitment that you must never forsake, and they frown upon divorce. This isn't God's will. If your marriage is hopeless, and if you and your partner are always fighting and unhappy, it's better to break up than to live a lie. There are some marriages that can't be saved . . . where the partners are irreconcilable. When two people are constantly arguing and resent each other, they're already divorced. I've talked to couples who've been virtually divorced for 50 years, yet are still living together. They're divorced from harmony, beauty, love, peace, kindness, and goodwill. They broke their marriage vows long ago.

Don't ever keep a bad promise, and don't compromise with anything evil or negative. Insist on Divine right action. Expect the best, and the best will come to you. There's nothing too good to be true or too wonderful to last because the love, light, and glory of the Infinite are the same yesterday, today, and forever.

If you say, "It's too good to be true," you're making a law for yourself and will have to live with the results of your thought. If you proclaim, "It can't last," *what* can't last? Love is ageless and timeless. So are peace, abundance, security, and inspiration. The truths of God are eternal and immutable.

⊶✦⊷

When you pray, you become a spiritual paratrooper as you fly above the problem or difficulty to the God Presence within. In that secret place where you walk and talk with God, you contemplate the Divine within you. Heaven is the Infinite Intelligence in you— where you live, move, and have your being. Focus on the All-Wise One, realizing that the answer is there and knowing in your heart and soul that the Almighty Power will respond to you. Then the day will break for you and all the shadows will flee. You must never dwell on the problem. Instead, detach your mind from that altogether and contemplate the solution; the way things ought to be; and the wholeness, beauty, and perfection of the Infinite.

⊶✦⊷

When Jonathan had flown better than any seagull on Earth, he thought that the others would be wild with joy because of his breakthrough. He exclaimed, "How much more there is now to living! Instead of our drab existence scrambling for fish, there's a reason to live. We can lift ourselves out of ignorance. We can realize that we're creatures of excellence, intelligence, and skill. We can be free. We can learn to fly!"

Yes, Infinite Spirit was within Jonathan, and It also works within you. The Divine Power has been described down through the ages by such enlightened beings as Buddha, Zoroaster, and Christ. The One Presence can lift you up from sickness, poverty, confusion, and frustration and lead you to the high road of happiness, peace of mind, and freedom. That Power is within you right now, and you can use It. You don't have to be like the flock or herd. What are *you* doing with your power of creative thought? Unfortunately, some people use it negatively and bring about misery, hardship, and suffering in their lives. Then they blame their problems on the devil or the "adversary."

The Bible says: "I will bring the blind by a way that they knew not; I will lead them in paths that they have not known." Millions are blind to the fact that thought is creative. Every thought is incipient action. What you feel, you attract; and what you imagine, you become. Any idea—whether good or bad—that you plant in your subconscious comes to pass as form, experiences, and events. There's a Supreme Intelligence within you that responds to your thought. So many people don't know this—they think that God is up in the sky somewhere.

⇥✛⇤

As I've described, the seagulls weren't happy about Jonathan's breakthrough experience. Instead, they ostracized him. You're familiar with that, aren't you? I talk to individuals who've started to study New Thought teachings and receive strong criticism from their family members. One mother wrote to her daughter: "The lake of fire is waiting for you. You've left the faith of your fathers and will be cursed. You're going to go to hell. Come back to the faith." This woman wasn't writing from a place of love, peace, or harmony. If you care about someone, you don't want them to burn for all eternity. You must have a frightful state of mind and be really sick to wish that any person in this world would burn forever and ever.

Now, you mustn't resent your mom, dad, or other relatives. They're reacting from the standpoint of ignorance, fear, and superstition. They've been brainwashed. To understand all is to forgive all. You can also try to enlighten them. You can ask, "Aren't you glad that I've found peace, harmony, and love in my life . . . something that gives me strength and a new zest for living?"

However, many people have closed minds and don't want to hear anything. In these cases, don't cast your pearls before swine. In other words, don't try to convert those who resist new ideas—they'll only resent you. When they're ready, they'll listen.

God waits for everybody because He's love. You also shouldn't be in any hurry to get others to change their views. Whether they're beggars, murderers, or religious leaders, all people shall awaken to see the transcendent glory of Infinite Spirit. Therefore, what's the rush? Surely the truth is offered to everyone. I've taught this in my radio programs, sermons, and books. Some say, "That's frightful," and write me letters telling me that I'm going to burn in hell for telling people that the Savior is within them and that each of us fashions our own destiny. However, I'll continue to say it because it's absolutely true.

꙳✠꙳

As Jonathan discovered, new ideas are often met with resistance. For instance, when the automobile was developed, there were riots in Dublin because the horse-and-buggy drivers thought that they'd be put out of business. In the history of the world, you'll read about the opposition to each great idea that was introduced. People fight the truth. They say that the "old religion" is good enough for them. What's good enough for *you?* Nothing's too good to be true. All the truths of God are within you, and what's true of the Infinite Presence is true of you. You're here to manifest all of the qualities and attributes of God. You're here to glorify Him—not to eat, sleep, or watch TV. How wonderful you are! Discover the powers that are within you, for God is the giver *and* the gift within.

꙳✠꙳

Once Jonathan was banished to the far cliffs, he was visited by two wise gulls, who represent the inspiration, guidance, creative ideas, and answers that come to you. You should entertain these promptings from heaven, for they're the voice of the Divine. They're the ideas that well up from the subliminal depths. Unfortunately, many people brush them aside, but that's like hanging an anchor from your neck and jumping into the ocean. Why? Because when you ignore the inspiration and whisperings of the God Presence, you drown in grief and frustration.

God is always knocking at your door saying, "Let me in." Why don't you open the door of your heart to the soft presence of the Unseen Guest? It opens with an inner latch. Infinite Spirit says: "I'll wipe away all your tears and will heal you. I'll inspire you and set you on the high road. I'll do wonderful things for you. I'm the Mighty God, your Everlasting Father." Yes, entertain these angels or inspirations that come to you

⊨✛⊨

After Jonathan was banished from the flock, he realized that heaven was within himself. Paradise is your mind at peace and that Invisible Intelligence in which you live, move, and have your being. The most important thing in living is to reach out for what you love. Then you'll move from glory to glory and from strength to strength. There's no end to the magnificence within you.

You can't be less tomorrow than you are today. Life doesn't go backward nor tarries with yesterday. Life is progression and endless development. Never in eternity could you exhaust the wonders and beauties that are within you. That's how amazing you are, for the kingdom of God is within you.

Learn everything you can about the treasures of heaven. The eternal truths of God are all you can take with you to the next world. You can't take your bank accounts with you. The precious things are in your own mind, where moths and rust can't consume them and where thieves can't break in and steal them. Take your knowledge of God, love, faith, and confidence with you; and you'll meet your loved ones in the next dimension, of course.

When you came into this world, you were met by loving hands, and when you go into the next one, your loved ones will welcome you there, too.

We mustn't think of death as an ending but as a new birthday in God. Our spirit lives on forever. A child who is dies in the womb still lives as a grace note in that grand symphony of all creation. We're *all* held together by that symphony of love. And Jesus, Moses, Buddha, and Mohammed are the great conductors of this universal, celestial orchestra.

⚜

When Jonathan went to live in the higher plane of existence after being exiled from his flock, he met the wisest seagull, Chiang, who taught him that he could escape the limits of the three-dimensional body and travel instantly wherever he liked because he was spirit. This means that someone who's fully illumined and inspired can go the next dimension or any plane. The Divine within that creates all things will project a body for that soul that meets the requirements of whatever environment he or she visits.

Uri Geller, the famous psychic who's able to bend spoons using mental powers, shows us that indeed the mind can do anything. Believe you have it now, and you shall receive it. The reality, of course, is the thought-image in your mind. You're spirit, and you can go through closed doors and collapse time and space if you learn how. Down through the ages, many swamis in Asia have been reported to have this capacity.

⚜

Never in eternity could you exhaust the wonders and the glories that are within you. God dwells in everybody, and love is seeing that Presence in everyone. When love comes in, everything unlike it exits. Look with understanding. Find out what you already know inside, and you'll see the way to fly—now and forevermore.

In a Nutshell

In prayer therapy, you're taught to lift your consciousness above the problem. If you raise your thoughts high enough, the difficulty will be solved. Withdraw your attention from the problem and concentrate gently on the Infinite Presence and Power that knows only the answer. As you do so, the solution will come. You're reaching a great state of consciousness.

We're all unique. We each have different fingerprints, nervous systems, and dreams because God never repeats Himself. Therefore, why on earth should you try to conform to the ideas of others?

Millions are blind to the fact that thought is creative and that every idea is incipient action. What you feel, you attract; and what you imagine, you become. Any idea—good or bad—that you plant in your subconscious comes to pass as form, experiences, and events. There's a Supreme Intelligence within you that responds to your thought.

Insist on Divine right action. Expect the best, and the best will come to you. Nothing is too good to be true or too wonderful to last, for the love, light, and glory of the Infinite are the same yesterday, today, and forever.

There's a Power within you that's been known down through the ages. This Divine Presence can lift you up from sickness, poverty, confusion, and frustration and lead you to the high road of happiness, peace of mind, and freedom. You have this Power within you right now, and you can use It constructively. You don't have to be like the flock or herd.

We shouldn't think of death as an ending but as a new birthday in God. If a loved one has passed on, we can rejoice in a new beginning in God. There's no end to our glory.

Chapter Twelve

Religion and Women's Bondage

Why did I include a special chapter on women in a book about self-confidence and self-esteem? Because, unfortunately, there are still many people who think that women are inferior to men and, indeed, ordained by the Bible to take a secondary place. Believing this, many women have accepted a lower status in life than they should and have low self-esteem. To illustrate, a woman came to me very upset. She firmly believed that she was called to be a minister, but was told by her father that biblical teachings opposed women becoming church leaders. He quoted the following verses from the New Testament: "Let your women keep silent in the churches, for they are not permitted to speak; but they are to be submissive. And if they want to learn something, let them ask their own husbands at home; for it is shameful for women to speak in church."

This literal interpretation of the Bible has kept women in bondage for thousands of years. So many people have forgotten the spirit or real meaning of the holy writings. The words *woman* and *man* in the Bible have nothing to do with the sex or gender of a person. Instead, *woman* refers to the subconscious, where Infinite Intelligence abides, while *man* refers to the conscious mind. Everyone has these male and female aspects in themselves.

When you read in the Bible that the women should obey men, don't take it literally. It means that the subconscious serves the conscious mind faithfully and gives form to that which is impressed upon it. Whatever ideas are "emotionalized" and felt as true sink into the subconscious and are brought forth as form, experiences, and events. The subconscious or female aspect doesn't respond to mental coercion or force—it responds to your emotional nature and accepts whatever you predominantly believe in your conscious mind. It acts on your convictions.

Your subconscious doesn't speak or articulate like your conscious mind—it simply brings forth the ideas it receives from the conscious mind. That's why it's written: "For they are not permitted to speak." This doesn't literally mean that women shouldn't speak. Similarly, the phrase "If they want to learn something, let them ask their own husbands at home" is figurative. The Infinite Intelligence within you is your husband; and you're to turn to It for guidance, right action, inspiration, and direction.

After I explained all of this to the woman who wanted to be a minister, she completely rejected the false interpretation of the Bible her father had given her and proceeded with her plans. Fortunately, in growing areas of the world, the Bible is now being taught from a metaphysical standpoint, and women are gaining their freedom from ignorant interpretations of the scriptures.

⊶✝⊷

Since the subconscious is completely receptive, when you pray scientifically for another person, you don't try to coerce it to obey your decrees. Instead, you quiet the mind and remain still and passive. Then your subconscious responds to your conviction regarding the Infinite Healing Presence within you. As well, in the prayer process, don't dwell on symptoms, aches, or pains. When you do affirmative treatments, you know that God is the author of peace and health—not the creator of sickness or confusion. For example, if you're praying for Betty Jones, affirm: "Betty Jones is known in Divine mind. God dwells within her, and His river of peace saturates her mind. His love fills her soul. God is, and His Presence flows through her, vitalizing, healing, and restoring her to wholeness and perfection. I give thanks for the Healing Power of God acting through Betty now."

In this prayer process, you identify with the Divine Presence in Betty, and you claim that what's true of God is true of her. After you complete the spiritual treatment, dismiss the matter until you feel led to pray again. The next time you pray for her, you should do so as if you hadn't prayed before—with the same focus and intention. Each time you say a spiritual affirmation for Betty, you're reinforcing the idea of vitality, wholeness, and perfection for her. When you relax and enter into a psychic state, what you feel is true of Betty will be felt by her. Gradually or immediately—as the case may be—the idea of perfect health and energy will manifest in Betty.

☆✞☆

Men and women are equal in the eyes of God. Fortunately, some churches do recognize this. Since the early days of Phineas Parkhurst Quimby in the 19th century, we've had women ministers in Unity, Science of Mind, Divine Science, and all branches of the New Thought field. Recently women priests have been ordained in some of the Anglican provinces, including the Episcopal church in the United States. There are also now women rabbis in Jewish congregations, and today many of the students in Protestant and Jewish seminaries are women. It's only a matter of time until we have women priests and bishops in the Roman Catholic church. In fact, there were many famous women superiors in the convents of the Middle Ages. They were illumined and inspired and became so outstandingly brilliant that they far outshone the men of their day. These men became frightened and sought to take away power from these female luminaries. If these men had known the truth, they would have rejoiced and been exceedingly glad that members of their religious order had moved onward, upward, and godward. In disempowering women in the Catholic church, these male "leaders" hurt themselves and the church, for to inhibit and block another is to stymie your own progress and advancement.

In the political arena, women have served as presidents and prime ministers of countries including Israel, Great Britain, the Philippines, and India. There are also many women serving in various levels of government in the United States, including Congress and the Supreme Court. It's quite likely that at some time in the future, a woman will become President of the United States.

⊨✛⊨

When the Bible says that he who loves his wife loves himself, and the two shall become one flesh, it's referring to the mystery of the male and female principle within everyone: the law of mind. When your conscious mind and subconscious agree on anything, your prayer is always answered. If they agree on harmony, prosperity, success, and achievement, then those qualities will manifest in your life according to universal law. When the male and female aspects work harmoniously and peacefully—becoming "one flesh"—the result is health, wealth, happiness, and true expression.

Assume the feeling of being what you long to be, and you will become it. Walk in the light that's true.

You're not to impregnate yourself with the negative thoughts, fears, and false beliefs of the world. Rather, enthrone godlike ideas and eternal verities in your conscious mind. As you busy your mind with these constructive thought patterns and truths, your subconscious will respond accordingly. This applies whether you're male or female.

⊨✛⊨

The subconscious, or female aspect, is subservient to the conscious mind, or male aspect. All this means is that your conscious mind is the guardian of the threshold and should see to it that nothing enters into your subconscious that doesn't fill your soul with joy, faith, confidence, vitality, and enthusiasm. It doesn't mean that the conscious mind is superior. It controls and dominates your subconscious, but the two are essential. Your subconscious responds to the suggestions and dominant thoughts and imagery of your conscious mind, bringing them into form and experience.

꙳✞꙳

The Bible describes the eternal truths of life and isn't talking about men and women as such. The writers of the Bible understood the workings of the mind and were well acquainted with what today is called "abnormal psychology." For about three centuries, the teachers and leaders of early Christianity did great things, including performing miraculous healings. They were on fire with the truth. However, the great Roman emperor Constantine developed the early church into a vast organization, establishing rites, ceremonies, and dogmas. The church grew on the outside but began to die slowly on the inside.

This is true of all the religions of the world. Their priests, ministers, and leaders forget the real Source of all blessings and bounty, and instead invest too much importance in form, ceremony, and hierarchy, worshiping the created thing rather than the Creator. You should therefore always look to your own Divine center for the light and true wisdom rather than accept false, literal interpretations of the Bible or other religious texts.

The true church is within yourself. It's not contained in marble buildings or in rituals. Your own heart is the temple of the Living God, for the I *am*—the Infinite Presence—dwells within your depths. And this One Power will guide you in all things.

꙳✞꙳

The cause of all the misery and suffering in the world is the inharmonious interaction of the male and female principles within everyone. Therefore, contemplate whatever is true, just, lovely, and good. Focus on these things all day long.

※✚※

Marriage in the Bible is the union of your thoughts and emotions, which produces all the fruits of the Spirit: love, joy, peace, abundance, security, happiness, and vitality. If your thoughts are godlike, your heart will become a chalice for God's love. The real marriage in the Bible is your sense of oneness with God.

※✚※

Genesis tells the story of Adam and Eve in the garden of Eden. This story wasn't meant to be taken literally, but is an allegory with a metaphysical meaning. Adam and Eve represent your conscious mind and subconscious, respectively. The serpent in the garden is a symbol of your five senses, which trick you at times and perhaps tempt you to turn away from belief in the One Power. You shouldn't let yourself be governed by your sensory perceptions, however, for then you become impregnated with all sorts of false knowledge, fears, doubts, and negative suggestions.

When I was a boy, I asked the priest at my church where the garden of Eden was. He said that it was between the Tigris and the Euphrates and told me to ask no more questions. In fact, there never was an actual garden of Eden or a forbidden fruit that caused the "downfall" of man. The allegory is really saying that we all receive instructions and ideas when we're young and impressionable. Like seeds, these ideas develop in us and became fixed states of mind. Some of these ideas are based on fear and prejudices, while others are about having honesty, integrity, goodwill, and so on. Therefore, the tree of good and evil is within *yourself,* and as an adult, you're responsible for the kinds of seeds that you cultivate in your garden. The idea that God is going to punish you or that you're a sinner in the hands of an angry deity is a false belief. Remember that there's only One Power—not two, three, or a thousand.

※✚※

In Genesis, God tells Eve: "Your desire shall be for your husband, and he shall rule over you." It's absolutely stupid to take this literally, but many people have done so in order to justify keeping women in subjugation. What this statement really means is that your conscious mind rules your subconscious; that is, your subconscious is amenable and subservient to the suggestions of your conscious mind.

The law of mind can be used for good or for evil. When you use it constructively, harmoniously, and peacefully, people call it God, Allah, Brahma, health, or happiness. When you use it ignorantly or maliciously, people call it Satan, the devil, insanity, fear, ignorance, superstition, or sickness. In fact, there's only *One* Power and Presence, and good and evil are in your own mind. How are *you* using your powerful subconscious?

⊰✦⊱

The ancients taught that praying is like wooing a woman. You tell her how much you love and care about her, give her presents, and wish her well. You remain faithful to her, and eventually your relationship results in a happy marriage. In the same way, you nourish and love an idea in your mind. Gradually, it sinks into your subconscious or female aspect and grows like a seed. You're married to your idea, and this union creates an answer to your prayer.

⊰✦⊱

On one of my daily radio broadcasts, I said that if you want something, you should vividly picture it in your mind and feel the reality of it. For example, if you want to go on a cruise, you should visualize the event in the here and now, feeling yourself sitting on the deck, looking at the stars, and experiencing the ocean breeze on your face. You should dwell on the scene and make it so real in your mind that when you open your eyes after the meditation period, you're actually amazed that you're not on a ship. This is a sure sign that you've fixed the idea in your subconscious, and it will come to pass. Even though you don't have the money to take the trip now, if you succeed in impregnating your subconscious, your dream will surely come to pass in ways that you couldn't imagine.

One of my radio listeners is a secretary at a large corporation. She heard this show and began to do an affirmative prayer treatment every night for a cruise for herself. On the third night, she fell asleep affirming: "Trip, trip, trip." She awakened the next morning and had no further desire to pray about it because she'd succeeded in fixing the idea in her subconscious mind. The sequel was interesting. When she was discussing her retirement benefits with her financial advisor soon thereafter, she learned that she could juggle her investments in her retirement account to take a month-long cruise.

Her subconscious, the female aspect, gave birth or form to her idea. As she began to think about the trip, got maps of various countries, and became interested in visiting foreign ports, she engaged the power of her subconscious mind. She planted the seeds of her dream with enthusiasm and love, and the subjective mind brought it to pass in its own way.

⋈✟⋈

The subconscious can be polluted by ignorant, tyrannical, despotic, and egotistic thoughts. When the conscious mind entertains gangsters, assassins, and marauders in the form of evil, hateful thoughts, these befoul the subconscious and bring forth all manner of diseases and disorders. Some men and women use their conscious mind to create negative experiences.

If you don't govern and direct your emotional life, you'll respond to all the sundry dark thoughts, fears, and predictions of gloom and doom that bombard you night and day. Then these irrational emotions will propel you into negative action and reaction. In biblical language, you're committing adultery when you allow evil, hate, jealousy, resentment, or hostility into the bed of your mind.

-ᴴ✝ᴴ-

The answer to all problems is to keep your attention on God and all things good. Then you create a wonderful future for yourself. The conscious mind should be a guide and protector for the holy child, which is your awareness of the Power of God within you. Enthrone in your mind ideas of health, peace, and security, and you'll experience the union of your thought and feeling. When they're fused, God enters in, and you have the joy of the answered prayer. Let your heart become a chalice for God's love, and you'll bring forth a child, which is God, or good, on Earth.

The first step is to relax and become still and quiet. This peaceful attitude of mind prevents extraneous matters and false ideas from interfering with your mental absorption of your ideal. Furthermore, in this receptive state, effort is reduced to a minimum.

There's a wonderful Power within you that's capable of bringing you what you imagine and feel is true. Become aware of this God Presence within. You must *know* and *believe* that you're operating a law of mind—wistfully daydreaming about the things you'd like to possess won't attract them to you. Become convinced of your Divine Power and use your mind constructively to bring into manifestation that which you desire. You must have a definite, clear-cut vision of what you wish for. Imagine it clearly and vividly so that you give your subconscious something definite to act upon. The subconscious mind is the sensitive film upon which the picture is impressed. The subconscious develops the picture and sends it back to you in a material form. Generally speaking, the more focused your attention is and the more time you spend exposing your film to the image you desire, the more perfect the answer to your prayer will be.

To believe is to be alive to the truths of God. As you sustain your belief, you'll experience the joy of an answered prayer. Accept the fact that you have an inner, creative power. Let it be a positive conviction. The Infinite Power is responsive to your thought. To know, understand, and apply this principle causes doubt, fear, and worry to gradually disappear. Remember that the deeper mind is responsive to your thought and that it manifests your habitual thinking and imagery all day long.

You should make it a special point to do the things you love. And if you're wondering what those are, realize that there's an Infinite Intelligence within you that knows only the answer. Say: "Infinite Intelligence reveals to me my true place in life, where I am doing what I love to do and am Divinely happy and prospered. And I follow the lead that comes clearly into my conscious, reasoning mind." As you do this, the answer will be revealed to you—it will be impossible for you to miss it. Then you'll follow the lead that comes to you and will discover that all your ways are pleasant and all your paths are peaceful.

In a Nutshell

The terms *man* and *woman* in the Bible refer to your conscious mind and subconscious, where the Infinite Intelligence abides. We all contain these male and female aspects.

You shouldn't impregnate yourself with the negative thoughts, fears, and false beliefs of the world. Instead, enthrone godlike ideas and eternal verities in your conscious mind. As you busy your mind with these constructive thought patterns and truths, your subconscious will respond accordingly. This law of mind applies to everyone, whether they're male or female.

There's only One Power. When you use It constructively, harmoniously, and peacefully, people call It God, Allah, Brahma, health, or happiness. When you use that Power ignorantly, stupidly, or maliciously, people call It Satan, the devil, insanity, fear, ignorance, superstition, and sickness. Therefore, good and evil are in your own mind. How are *you* using the Almighty Source within?

You're not just a physical body: You're a mental and spiritual being. Your body is a vehicle and a representation of your thoughts, feelings, imagination, and beliefs. The Living Spirit is the essence of every person.

Plant the seeds of joy, harmony, and love in your subconscious mind; and you'll bring forth health, peace, strength, and security. Marriage in the Bible is the union of thought and feeling. When they're fused, the third element—God—enters in, and you experience the joy of the answered prayer. Let your heart become a chalice for God's love.

⋇ ⋇

Biography of Joseph Murphy

Joseph Murphy was born on May 20, 1898, in a small town in the County of Cork, Ireland. His father, Denis Murphy, was a deacon and professor at the National School of Ireland, a Jesuit facility. His mother, Ellen, née Connelly, was a housewife, who later gave birth to another son, John, and a daughter, Catherine.

Joseph was brought up in a strict Catholic household. His father was quite devout and, indeed, was one of the few lay professors who taught Jesuit seminarians. He had a broad knowledge of many subjects and developed in his son the desire to study and learn.

Ireland at that time was suffering from one of its many economic depressions, and many families were starving. Although Denis Murphy was steadily employed, his income was barely enough to sustain the family.

Young Joseph was enrolled in the National School and was a brilliant student. He was encouraged to study for the priesthood and was accepted as a Jesuit seminarian. However, by the time he reached his late teen years, he began to question the Catholic orthodoxy of the Jesuits, and he withdrew from the seminary. Since his goal was to explore new ideas and gain new experiences—a goal he couldn't pursue in Catholic-dominated Ireland—he left his family to go to America.

He arrived at the Ellis Island Immigration Center with only $5 in his pocket. His first project was to find a place to live. He was fortunate to locate a rooming house where he shared a room with a pharmacist who worked in a local drugstore.

Joseph's knowledge of English was minimal, as Gaelic was spoken both in his home and at school, so like most Irish immigrants, Joseph worked as a day laborer, earning enough to keep himself fed and housed.

He and his roommate became good friends, and when a job opened up at the drugstore where his friend worked, he was hired to be an assistant to the pharmacist. He immediately enrolled in a school to study pharmacy. With his keen mind and desire to learn, it didn't take long before Joseph passed the qualification exams and became a full-fledged pharmacist. He now made enough money to rent his own apartment. After a few years, he purchased the drugstore, and for the next few years ran a successful business.

When the United States entered World War II, Joseph enlisted in the Army and was assigned to work as a pharmacist in the medical unit of the 88th Infantry Division. At that time, he renewed his interest in religion and began to read extensively about various spiritual beliefs. After his discharge from the Army, he chose not to return to his career in pharmacy. He traveled extensively, taking courses in several universities both in the United States and abroad.

From his studies, Joseph became enraptured with the various Asian religions and went to India to learn about them in depth. He studied all of the major faiths and their histories. He extended these studies to the great philosophers from ancient times until the present.

Although he studied with some of the most intelligent and farsighted professors, the one person who most influenced Joseph was Dr. Thomas Troward, who was a judge as well as a philosopher, doctor, and professor. Judge Troward became Joseph's mentor and introduced him to the study of philosophy, theology, and law as well as mysticism and the Masonic order. Joseph became an active member of this order, and over the years rose in the Masonic ranks to the 32nd degree in the Scottish Rite.

Upon his return to the United States, Joseph chose to become a minister and bring his broad knowledge to the public. As his concept of Christianity was not traditional and indeed ran counter to most of the Christian denominations, he founded his own church in Los Angeles. He attracted a small number of congregants, but it did not take long for his message of optimism and hope rather than the "sin-and-damnation" sermons of so many ministers to attract many men and women to his church.

Dr. Joseph Murphy was a proponent of the New Thought movement. This movement was developed in the late 19th and early 20th centuries by many philosophers and deep thinkers who studied this phenomenon and preached, wrote, and practiced a new way of looking at life. By combining a metaphysical, spiritual, and pragmatic approach to the way we think and live, they uncovered the secret of attaining what we truly desire.

The proponents of the New Thought movement preached a new idea of life that is based on practical, spiritual principles that we can all use to enrich our lives and created perfected results. We can do these things only as we have found the law and worked out the understanding of the law, which God seems to have written in riddles in the past.

Of course, Dr. Murphy wasn't the only minister to preach this positive message. Several churches, whose ministers and congregants were influenced by the New Thought movement, were founded and developed in the decades following World War II. The Church of Religious Science, Unity Church, and other places of worship preach philosophies similar to this. Dr. Murphy named his organization The Church of Divine Science. He often shared platforms, conducted joint programs with his like-minded colleagues, and trained other men and women to join his ministry.

Over the years, other churches joined with him in developing an organization called the Federation of Divine Science, which serves as an umbrella for all Divine Science churches. Each of the Divine Science church leaders continues to push for more education, and Dr. Murphy was one of the leaders who supported the creation of the Divine Science School in St. Louis, Missouri, to train new ministers and provide ongoing education for both ministers and congregants.

The annual meeting of the Divine Science ministers was a must to attend, and Dr. Murphy was a featured speaker at this event. He encouraged the participants to study and continue to learn, particularly about the importance of the subconscious mind.

Over the next few years, Murphy's local Church of Divine Science grew so large that his building was too small to hold them. He rented The Wilshire Ebell Theater, a former movie theater. His services were so well attended that even this venue could not always accommodate all who wished to attend. Classes conducted by Dr. Murphy and his staff supplemented his Sunday services that were attended by 1,300 to 1,500 people. Seminars and lectures were held most days and evenings. The church remained at the Wilshire Ebell Theater in Los Angeles until 1976, when it moved to a new location in Laguna Hills, California.

To reach the vast numbers of people who wanted to hear his message, Dr. Murphy also created a weekly radio talk show, which eventually reached an audience of over a million listeners. Many of his followers suggested that he tape his lectures and radio programs. He was at first reluctant to do so, but agreed to experiment. His radio programs were recorded on extra-large 78-rpm discs, a common practice at that time. He had six cassettes made from one of these discs and placed them on the information table in the lobby of the Wilshire Ebell Theater. They sold out the first hour. This started a new venture. His tapes of his lectures explaining biblical texts, and providing meditations and prayers for his listeners, were not only sold in his church, but in other churches and bookstores and via mail order.

As the church grew, Dr. Murphy added a staff of professional and administrative personnel to assist him in the many programs in which he was involved and in researching and preparing his first books. One of the most effective members of his staff was his administrative secretary, Dr. Jean Wright. Their working relationship developed into a romance, and they were married—a lifelong partnership that enriched both of their lives.

At this time (the 1950s), there were very few major publishers of spiritually inspired material. The Murphys located some small publishers in the Los Angeles area, and worked with them to produce a series of small books (often 30 to 50 pages printed in pamphlet form) that were sold, mostly in churches, from $1.50 to $3.00 per book. When the orders for these books increased to the point where they required second and third printings, major publishers recognized that there was a market for such books and added them to their catalogs.

Dr. Murphy became well known outside of the Los Angeles area as a result of his books, tapes, and radio broadcasts, and was invited to lecture all over the country. He did not limit his lectures to religious matters, but spoke on the historical values of life, the art of wholesome living, and the teachings of great philosophers—from both Eastern and Western cultures.

As Dr. Murphy never learned to drive, he had to arrange for somebody to drive him to the various places where he was invited to lecture in his very busy schedule. One of Jean's functions as his administrative secretary and later as his wife was to plan his assignments and arrange for trains or flights, airport pickups, hotel accommodations, and all the other details of the trips.

The Murphys traveled frequently to many countries around the world. One of his favorite working vacations was to hold seminars on cruise ships. These trips lasted a week or more and would take him to many countries around the world. In his lectures, he emphasized the importance of understanding the power of the subconscious mind and the life principles based on belief in the one God, the "I AM."

One of Dr. Murphy's most rewarding activities was speaking to the inmates at many prisons. Many ex-convicts wrote him over the years, telling him how his words had truly turned their lives around and inspired them to live spiritual and meaningful lives.

Dr. Murphy's pamphlet-sized books were so popular that he began to expand them into more detailed and longer works. His wife gave us some insight into his manner and method of writing. She reported that he wrote his manuscripts on a tablet and pressed so hard on his pencil or pen that you could read the imprint on the next page. He seemed to be in a trance while writing. He would remain in his office for four to six hours without disturbance until he stopped and said that was enough for the day. Each day was the same. He never went back into the office again until the next morning to finish what he'd started. He took no food or drink while he was working, He was just alone with his thoughts and his huge library of books, to which he referred from time to time. His wife sheltered him from visitors and calls and took care of church business and other activities.

Dr. Murphy was always looking for simple ways to discuss the issues and to elaborate points. He chose some of his lectures to present on cassettes, records, or CDs, as technologies developed in the audio field.

His entire collection of CDs and cassettes are tools that can be used for most problems that individuals encounter in life. His basic theme is that the solution to problems lies within you. Outside elements cannot change your thinking. That is, your mind is your own. To live a better life, it's your mind, not outside circumstances, that you must change. You create your own destiny. The power of change is in your mind, and by using the power of your subconscious mind, you can make changes for the better.

Dr. Murphy wrote more than 30 books. His most famous work, *The Power of the Unconscious Mind,* which was first published in 1963, became an immediate bestseller. It was acclaimed as one of the best self-help guides ever written. Millions of copies have been sold and continue to be sold all over the world.

Among some of his other best-selling books were *Telepsychics— The Magic Power of Perfect Living, The Amazing Laws of Cosmic Mind, Secrets of the I-Ching, The Miracle of Mind Dynamics, Your Infinite Power to Be Rich,* and *The Cosmic Power Within You.*

Dr. Murphy died in December 1981, and his wife, Dr. Jean Murphy, continued his ministry after his death. In a lecture she gave in 1986, quoting her late husband, she reiterated his philosophy:

I want to teach men and women of their Divine Origin, and the powers regnant within them. I want to inform that this power is within and that they are their own saviors and capable of achieving their own salvation. This is the message of the Bible and nine-tenths of our confusion today is due to wrongful, literal interpretation of the life-transforming truths offered in it.

I want to reach the majority, the man on the street, the woman overburdened with duty and suppression of her talents and abilities. I want to help others at every stage or level of consciousness to learn of the wonders within.

She said of her husband: "He was a practical mystic, possessed by the intellect of a scholar, the mind of a successful executive, the heart of the poet." His message summed up was: "You are the king, the ruler of your world, for you are one with God."

⊰✞⊱ ⊰✞⊱

Notes

Notes

Notes

Notes

Notes

Notes

Notes

Notes

Notes

Notes

Notes

Notes

HAY HOUSE TITLES OF RELATED INTEREST

YOU CAN HEAL YOUR LIFE, the movie, starring Louise L. Hay &
Friends (available as a 1-DVD program and an expanded 2-DVD set)
Watch the trailer at: **www.LouiseHayMovie.com**

⌗✦⌗

CALM: A Proven Four-Step Process Designed
Specifically for Women Who Worry,* by Denise Marek

*THE POWER OF A SINGLE THOUGHT: How to Initiate
Major Life Changes from the Quiet of Your Mind* (book-with-CD),
revised and edited by Gay Hendricks and Debbie DeVoe

*THE POWER OF INTENTION: Learning to Co-create
Your World Your Way,* by Dr. Wayne W. Dyer

*10 STEPS TO TAKE CHARGE OF YOUR EMOTIONAL LIFE:
Overcoming Anxiety, Distress, and Depression Through Whole-Person Healing,*
by Eve A. Wood, M.D.

*WHAT TO DO WHEN YOU DON'T KNOW WHAT TO DO:
Common Horse Sense,* by Wyatt Webb

⌗✦⌗

All of the above are available at your
local bookstore, or may be ordered by contacting:

Hay House USA: **www.hayhouse.com**®
Hay House Australia: **www.hayhouse.com.au**
Hay House UK: **www.hayhouse.co.uk**
Hay House South Africa: **orders@psdprom.co.za**
Hay House India: **www.hayhouseindia.co.in**

⌗✦⌗

※✛※

We hope you enjoyed this Hay House book.
If you'd like to receive a free catalog featuring additional
Hay House books and products, or if you'd like
information about the Hay Foundation, please contact:

HAY
HOUSE

Hay House, Inc.
P.O. Box 5100
Carlsbad, CA 92018-5100

(760) 431-7695 or **(800) 654-5126**
(760) 431-6948 (fax) or **(800) 650-5115 (fax)**
www.hayhouse.com® • **www.hayfoundation.org**

※✛※

Published and distributed in Australia by: Hay House Australia Pty. Ltd.,
18/36 Ralph St., Alexandria NSW 2015 • *Phone:* 612-9669-4299
Fax: 612-9669-4144 • www.hayhouse.com.au

Published and distributed in the United Kingdom by: Hay House UK, Ltd.,
292B Kensal Rd., London W10 5BE • *Phone:* 44-20-8962-1230
Fax: 44-20-8962-1239 • www.hayhouse.co.uk

Published and distributed in the Republic of South Africa by: Hay House SA
(Pty), Ltd., P.O. Box 990, Witkoppen 2068 • *Phone/Fax:* 27-11-467-8904
orders@psdprom.co.za • www.hayhouse.co.za

Published in India by: Hay House Publishers India, Muskaan Complex,
Plot No. 3, B-2, Vasant Kunj, New Delhi 110 070 • *Phone:* 91-11-4176-1620
Fax: 91-11-4176-1630 • www.hayhouse.co.in

Distributed in Canada by: Raincoast, 9050 Shaughnessy St., Vancouver, B.C.
V6P 6E5 • *Phone:* (604) 323-7100 • *Fax:* (604) 323-2600 • www.raincoast.com

※✛※

Tune in to **HayHouseRadio.com®** for the best in inspirational
talk radio featuring top Hay House authors! And, sign up via the
Hay House USA Website to receive the Hay House online newsletter
and stay informed about what's going on with your favorite authors.
You'll receive bimonthly announcements about: Discounts and Offers,
Special Events, Product Highlights, Free Excerpts, Giveaways, and more!
www.hayhouse.com®